# The Journey of the Soul Through the Seven Major Chakras

*Inspirational Spiritual Writings*

## ASTRA FERRO

BALBOA PRESS
A DIVISION OF HAY HOUSE

Copyright © 2019 Astra Ferro.

All rights reserved. No part of this book may be used or reproduced by any means, graphic, electronic, or mechanical, including photocopying, recording, taping or by any information storage retrieval system without the written permission of the author except in the case of brief quotations embodied in critical articles and reviews.

Balboa Press books may be ordered through booksellers or by contacting:

Balboa Press
A Division of Hay House
1663 Liberty Drive
Bloomington, IN 47403
www.balboapress.com
1 (877) 407-4847

Because of the dynamic nature of the Internet, any web addresses or links contained in this book may have changed since publication and may no longer be valid. The views expressed in this work are solely those of the author and do not necessarily reflect the views of the publisher, and the publisher hereby disclaims any responsibility for them.

The author of this book does not dispense medical advice or prescribe the use of any technique as a form of treatment for physical, emotional, or medical problems without the advice of a physician, either directly or indirectly. The intent of the author is only to offer information of a general nature to help you in your quest for emotional and spiritual well-being. In the event you use any of the information in this book for yourself, which is your constitutional right, the author and the publisher assume no responsibility for your actions.

Any people depicted in stock imagery provided by Getty Images are models, and such images are being used for illustrative purposes only.
Certain stock imagery © Getty Images.

Print information available on the last page.

ISBN: 978-1-9822-2857-6 (sc)
ISBN: 978-1-9822-2859-0 (hc)
ISBN: 978-1-9822-2858-3 (e)

Library of Congress Control Number: 2019907016

Balboa Press rev. date: 06/06/2019

# Dedication

*I dedicate this book to my Teachers and Master in Spirit, and to the Ancestral Group Soul, Companions of Old, who have guided, supported and helped me over so many years. Their wisdom, guidance and love and their infinite patience have been the guiding Light in my journey of soul understanding.*

# Acknowledgement

Along my own journey, my search for the Truth, I am deeply grateful for the spiritual teachings that have been instrumental in helping me to move forward along the stepping stones of my own Path. Since I was a child, I have always looked upon the Master Jesus as a very special shining Light in my world. In my adulthood, I am deeply grateful to those Teachings that have inspired me to move forward along the spiritual Path.

I especially would like to pay tribute to:
    The Teachings of the Master Djwhal Khul
    The Philosophy of the Buddha
    The Teachings of White Eagle
    Henry Thomas Hamblin
    Joel Goldsmith

# Foreword

*The Journey of the Soul Through the Seven Major Chakras*, is a deep and inspiring explanation of the experiences we all go through as we learn lessons and unfold and develop our innate spiritual qualities. If you are looking for clear and inspiring teaching, this book will lead you through ever deeper understanding of your chakras and unfold many other aspects of spiritual teaching that will help and inspire you in your journey through incarnations.

Astra's knowledge and clear insightful teaching is invaluable to anyone seeking to understand their karma. She takes us through our experiences in lifetime after lifetime and gives us guidance through those experiences we have chosen. Astra explains how in each incarnation we encounter lessons and teachers that correspond to our chakras as we raise the Christ consciousness within us. It is wonderful to have a book which helps us understand what is happening as we progress; to understand the effect and relevance of the major Rays of Creation, and the initiations we move through.

For those seeking not only to understand their karma, but also to make sense of their current challenges, this book will be an invaluable guide, giving insight into how their soul has used various incarnations, how some qualities have been veiled for this lifetime, how some have been thrown into relief, but above all the innate and powerful strength we can each access – the deep Christ Light within us – and how we can be sure that this can survive and overcome everything, incarnation after incarnation.

This book will give hope, perspective, enlightenment and meaning to your life's journey and I commend it to you.

Rose Elliot, MBE D.Litt. (Hon). DFAstrol.S, QHP
Author of *'I met a Monk'* and *'Every Breath You Take'*

# Contents

Dedication ................................................................................. v
Acknowledgement ................................................................ vii
Foreword ................................................................................. ix
Glossary ................................................................................ xiii
Diagrams:
    Chart of Influences & Links of the Seven Major Chakras ...... xvii
    Chart of Seven Major Chakras ................................................ xix
Author's Note ...................................................................... xxi
    What this book is about ...................................................... xxv

Chapter 1    The Personality ................................................ 1
Chapter 2    The Soul, The Bridge, The Antahkarana ......................... 7
Chapter 3    Explanation of the Chakras or Centres In The Body ........ 11
Chapter 4    Explanation of the Seven Major Rays ............................ 14
Chapter 5    Explanation of the Initiations ........................................ 22
Chapter 6    Explanation of the Colours ............................................ 32
Chapter 7    Let us go through the Chakras ...................................... 35
    The First Chakra is the Root – Our Foundation ................... 35
    The Second Chakra is the Sacral ......................................... 44
    The Third Chakra is the Solar Plexus .................................. 52
    The Fourth Chakra is the Heart ........................................... 62
    The Fifth Chakra is the Throat ............................................ 75
    The Sixth Chakra is the Brow .............................................. 87
    The Seventh Chakra is the Crown ....................................... 96
Chapter 8    Where does karma fit into all this? ............................... 104
Chapter 9    Healing with the Ancestors .......................................... 118
Chapter 10  The Spirit ..................................................................... 126
Chapter 11  ….and so the journey continues… ............................... 128

# Glossary of Terms Used Throughout this Book

**Absolute Being**

Also, called the Creator. Some may call this Being God as it is exemplified by orthodoxy. However, when I refer to the Absolute Being in this book, I mean *The* Absolute Being - above creation and beyond orthodoxy terminology. This can also be described as 'the Breath', 'the Force', 'the Energy' that sustains all life.

**Ages**

Our soul lessons take us through the 12 signs of the Zodiac and in the greater Cycle each sign is described as an Age. For instance, currently on earth we are leaving the Piscean Age and entering the Aquarian Age. Both Ages are very much influencing events around the globe. An Age is approximately 2,400 years.

**Akashic**

These are known as accurate and true records which are imprinted in the ether as our soul goes through earthly life's experiences. Each time our soul learns a lesson it is automatically imprinted in the Akashic records. This can never be incorrect – as our soul learns, so it is written. It is also known as life-time review.

**Ancestral Group Soul**

For many years I have worked with the Ancestral Group Soul to help and support people who come to me for counselling and guidance. I was made aware of these group of souls in spirit many years ago and slowly over the years have come to know and trust them. These are souls in spirit, companions of old, whose mission is to help us understand our path, give us insight into past lives and why certain issues and problems keep coming up again and again. They seek nothing but are simply happy to assist when we ask. They are not necessarily family members.

**Antahkarana**

This is the Bridge that connects the lower to the higher, the Personality to the Soul, and the Soul to the Spirit.

**Atmic**

This is the highest level after the Buddhic consciousness. Only those who have attained the very high degrees of initiation are aware of this level.

**Buddhic**

A state of consciousness which is attained once we have gone through the emotional and mental planes. When we reach this level, we would have found enlightenment.

**Devas**

These beings are on a different life stream from the human more in line with the Angelic and Natural Kingdom They help humans as do those of the Angelic and Natural Kingdom.

### Etheric

The next level after the physical. We all have an etheric body which is a replica of the physical but without all the restraints, emotions and thoughts of the human body.

### Kundalini

This is Divine energy located at the base of the spine (Root Chakra) which raises up the spine to the Crown, when the Soul has learned its lessons and unfolded to the highest degree. It is very powerful and should not be forced. The kundalini will raise itself when the Soul is ready.

### Logos/Logoi

This is another name for Gods who are responsible for different universal systems, i.e. there is a Planetary Logos, a Solar Logos and a Cosmic Logos in our specific Universe.

### Monad/Monadic

Again, referring to the highest – God or Atmic.

### OTT

Over the top – exaggeration

### Root-races

There are seven root races thus far known to humanity. These are:
    The Polarian
    The Hyperborean
    The Lemurian
    The Atlantean
    The Aryan (our current root-race)
    Two others as yet unnamed to follow

There are seven sub-races within each root-race. We are presently in the fifth sub-race of the Fifth Root Race.

**Shamballa**

This is said to be the etheric place where the Council of Masters meet and have their Ashrams. This is a place of great energy and power and it is from here that the energy of the Masters guiding our planet emanate. It is the centre where the Will of God is known.

# CHART OF INFLUENCES & LINKS OF THE SEVEN MAJOR CHAKRAS

| CHAKRA | RAY | ELEMENT | COLOUR | PLANET |
|---|---|---|---|---|
| Crown – Pineal Gland | 7th – Ceremonial Law & Order, Ritual | Thought, Wisdom | Violet | Neptune/Sun |
| Brow – Pituitary Gland | 6th – Devotion, Inspirational & Idealism | Light | Indigo | Uranus |
| Throat – Thyroid | 5th – Concrete Knowledge & Science | Ether | Blue | Mercury |
| Heart – Thymus Gland | 4th – Harmony Through Conflict | Air | Green | Venus/Sun |
| Solar Plexus – Pancreas | 3rd – Active Intelligence | Fire | Yellow | Jupiter |
| Sacral – The Gonads | 2nd – Love & Wisdom | Water | Orange | Mars/Moon |
| Root – Adrenal Glands | 1st – Will & Power | Earth | Red | Saturn |

The Chakras work through the emotional, mental and spiritual bodies. The seven chakras are aligned thus:

The Base of Spine to the Crown & Brow Chakra.

The Sacral Chakra to the Throat Chakra.

The Solar Plexus to the Heart Chakra.

It needs to be understood that the Seven Major Rays operate and influence more than one chakra at a time. The above is only a guidance.

# CHART OF SEVEN MAJOR CHAKRAS

| | | |
|---|---|---|
| *Crown Chakra* | | *Spirituality* |
| *Third Eye Chakra* | | *Awareness* |
| *Throat Chakra* | | *Communication* |
| *Heart Chakra* | | *Love, Healing* |
| *Solar Plexus Chakra* | | *Wisdom, Power* |
| *Sacral Chakra* | | *Sexuality, Creativity* |
| *Root Chakra* | | *Basic Trust* |

| | | |
|---|---|---|
| **Crown** | - | **I KNOW THAT I AM** |
| **Brow** | - | **I SEE** |
| **Throat** | - | **I SPEAK, I EXPRESS** |
| **Heart** | - | **I LOVE** |
| **Solar Plexus** | - | **I DO** |
| **Sacral** | - | **I FEEL** |
| **Root** | - | **I AM** |

# Author's Note

This book is about the journey of the soul as it travels through the seven major chakras. I was meditating one day, in the late summer of 2017, when I sensed and saw my spiritual Teacher who impressed upon me that I should go to Bhutan and Tibet. The reason why was not given but over many years I know that when my Teacher suddenly makes himself known to me and gives me a message, then I accept it. I started searching the internet for trips to Bhutan and Tibet. As I investigated, it became clear that what I was looking for was simply not there and the things I found did not feel right to me. However, one day a couple of weeks later, when browsing through Facebook, a friend of mine who is a very special spiritual man, indicated that he was taking a group to Bhutan later in the autumn. I immediately felt this was right for me, so I contacted him and lo and behold a couple of months later I was off to Bhutan.

The journey through Bhutan was without a doubt, the most challenging trip I have ever done. On the one hand it was incredibly physically challenging and at the same time it was the most spiritual uplifting and rewarding journey I have ever undertaken. Bhutan is a beautiful country. The landscape through the mountainous regions was breath-taking. The air was so pure. There is a vibration, an energy throughout Bhutan that is hard to explain – it just is. One feels the force of nature (Bhutan is over 70% forests) and an incredible sense of being at peace. Peace was the quality that was with me throughout. Peace of heart, peace of mind and stilled emotions. Physically I really went through the mill. In some areas I had problems breathing with the high altitude. A week before I had left for this trip, I had fallen down the stairs at home and sprained my right foot, so I needed to carry a walking stick and just as well as I certainly needed it. I found walking the terrain difficult physically and remain so grateful to the dear souls who were there with a helping arm. We travelled through Bhutan from east to west through very uneven roads, bumpy to say the least, and yet even with the physical discomfort there was an incredible upliftment of the heart as I gazed at the scenery around me. Bhutan is such a special and spiritual country.

Throughout this trip I had many wonderful spiritual experiences culminating in the Monastery in Punakha where we met Lama Dorji, a very special man with an amazing aura and presence. However, the most poignant realization for me was that this journey led me through my own seven major chakras. This had not been evident before the trip, but I realised when in Bhutan that this was the reason I had to go there. Although I could not go to Tibet we were close enough to its borders for me to meditate and receive spiritual insight.

Bhutan enabled me to process conditions within me from past lives that needed addressing and I had the opportunity for cleansing and clearing these. I can honestly say that the journey to Bhutan has changed my thinking and my feelings and has given me a clearer insight and vision into my own spiritual work. As a result, I am now facilitating the journey of other Souls, helping them to experience their own voyage through the seven major chakras. I am doing this through workshops and one to one counselling. I am learning so much through this process.

I often close my eyes and feel myself back there in that beautiful landscape. Words are not always easy to describe what I experienced, what I felt throughout and most importantly what I have brought back with me. I have been very blessed in my life to have travelled extensively and, in many places, I have had wonderful meditations and spiritual experiences. I have a particular and special affinity with Japan where I have facilitated many workshops over the years and also Hawaii and still remember the wonderful insight I received in Kauai three years ago which prompted me to retire from office work and continue my spiritual work. But I can honestly say no other country has affected me so deeply as Bhutan. I actually felt my chakras come alive throughout the journey and this has enabled me to understand myself better at a much deeper level than ever before.

It is because of this that I feel able to share my own experiences and my knowledge to help others understand themselves at that deeper level. Hence the start of this book and my counselling work with the chakras.

After the journey to Bhutan, in the summer of 2018, I was impressed once again by my Teacher to travel to Peru. This came through receiving information about a Retreat Centre in the Sacred Valley in Peru which had amazing Chakra Gardens. This wonderful Centre is called Willka Tika and I would really recommend a visit.

So, in December 2018 I made this journey, accompanied by my nephew Dominic. It was unlike anything I had ever experienced. Once again I encountered the physical challenges. The high altitude affected me severely in several places, namely, Cusco and Lake Titicaca. However, it was in Cusco where I had the most challenging time as I came face to face with past karma. The feelings of suppression, fear and oppression got to me and I had a couple of unpleasant nights dealing with all this. It did not help that the Hotel we stayed at had been an old monastery and most people were complaining of headaches and a bad night the following morning. The energy in the Hotel was so oppressive.

However, when we eventually got to Willka Tika, the Retreat Centre in the Sacred Valley, all changed, and I was met with a most peaceful and warm welcome. The Chakra gardens had been created with love and deep understanding and it was an absolutely joy for me to wander round the gardens and enjoy their fragrance and deep peace. Here was nature at its most beautiful. Each garden had meaning, and I spent hours meditating in them. I received wonderful insight into my journey, not just the current one but my whole life's journey.

One of our trips to sacred sites was of course to Macchu Picchu. The train journey was amazing. All the time I felt driven by a desire to get there fast, but not sure at the time why this should be. On arrival at Aguas Calientes, we proceeded to enter this special site. I had made it clear that I could not go up too high but would stay at the first level with a few others who, like me, could not undertake the higher climbs. However, our second guide allowed us time to rest before enticing us up little by little. To my surprise, I actually went up by more than two-thirds of the way, enjoying the beautiful scenery but, above all, intuitively sensing my connection with this remarkable place. Clearly, the Incas who constructed this citadel were incredible people. Once again I faced past karma but this time it was not unpleasant but rather I recalled a good life that I had experienced.

Both journeys in the last couple of years, first to Bhutan and then to Peru, have given me tremendous insight and understanding as to why the Soul's Journey through the Chakras is so meaningful. I needed these two journeys to attain a more profound knowledge of myself. I could not have written this book had it not been for those two profound journeys.

I invite you here to join me in this journey. The experiences may be challenging but you have the Light within, and the innate courage and strength to guide you forward.

As I write this book, I have just agreed to co-host a Workshop in Willka Tika, with owner and founder Carol Cumes. This is scheduled to take place in May 2020. This workshop will be about the Journey through the Seven Major Chakras, touching on past lives and healing with the Ancestors. I work with clients who have conditions, problems and issues that are often related to past lives – soul lessons not fully learned, deep impressions retained in the soul memory, or simply, karma that needs to be faced and cleared. In this work, I am helped by the Ancestral Group Soul, with whom I have had direct access and contact for many years. Willka Tika is just so right to facilitate this workshop with its amazing and wonderful Chakra gardens. There are dazzling arrays of flowers and exotic medicinal plants abound in the renowned Seven Sacred Chakra Gardens built for wellbeing, healing and meditation.

I look forward to my return and participate in the Andean ceremonies to heal and work with Pachamama.

# WHAT THIS BOOK IS ABOUT

Throughout my own experiences in life, teaching and counselling on soul understanding and soul healing, this journey through the Chakras has been the most deeply significant. It has brought together other aspects of my understanding of the Seven Major Rays and the Soul's Initiations. I can see how these are all related and play such a significant part in our understanding of ourselves, first as personality, then as Souls and also in our awareness of the pure essence, the Spirit within and of the Cosmos.

Often in my workshops, I talk about the three E's, namely:

- Experiment
- Experience
- Expression

I believe that all life is an experiment and it is through the Soul's journey and the experiences that we go through, lifetime after lifetime, that we learn to express the Spirit within us. Each lifetime brings us an opportunity to learn soul lessons and unfold spiritual qualities. In my previous book *'Stepping Stones on the Spiritual Path',* I speak about these qualities. Before incarnation the Soul chooses the blueprint for the experiences it needs to continue its journey. This may be hard for some people to accept, especially if their circumstances are harsh as they cannot believe they would choose such a life.

Between each lifetime on earth, a period called pralaya, the soul has the opportunity to look at its own akashic records (also known as life-times review) and note its progress, what lessons have been learned and which are still to be learned. The Soul chooses its time, together with its mentor or teacher, in which to return to earth to continue its journey.

The Soul's journey is about unfolding and developing its spiritual qualities through the experience of each incarnation. In each incarnation we encounter experiences to help us learn lessons corresponding to the chakras, the rays and the initiations that the Soul needs to complete before it reaches the ultimate – the raising of its Christ Consciousness to the fullest degree. I use the word Christ as a Universal Consciousness and not relating to any individual being.

Throughout my work I have come to understand how everything is so inter-related and inter-connected. We cannot just speak of the chakras without bringing in the understanding of the relationship with the Major Rays of Creation and the Great Initiations, both of the individual soul and of the Elements. Therefore, in this book I also bring my understanding of this deep relationship. During our journey, as we experience the lessons of the chakras, in particular and especially the 1$^{st}$, 2$^{nd}$ and 3$^{rd}$ chakras, related to the personality, we also accumulate Karma. I feel it is important to understand that karma is not a punishment but rather an opportunity to learn and therefore I am giving my understanding of karma in Chapter 8.

My work for many years has been that of working with the Ancestral Group Soul and in Chapter 9, I give more detailed explanation of how we can heal with the Ancestors. From the Ancestral Group Soul we derive our spiritual DNA.

The journey of the Path of the Soul is the greatest journey, the greatest adventure, we could ever take. It may be full of pitfalls and challenges, but it also shows us what courage and strength and perseverance there is inside each one of us. We may not always understand why we go through these experiences or what we are learning but nevertheless it is those experiences which makes us what we are. Right now, we are the sum total of all we have ever been, of all we have ever learned and unfolded. It may be that in each incarnation we may choose to veil some of our qualities or experiences from the past because that knowledge may not help us in our current challenges. In this book I describe what the Chakras, Rays and Initiations are about. There is a more detailed explanation about the chakras in the pages to come.

# CHAPTER 1

# The Personality

The personality is our outer character in this lifetime. Our personality is our likes and dislikes, our emotions, our thoughts. It is the image we portray to others in everyday life. Some may call it our character. Before awakening to the spiritual world, our personality is ruled by our emotions and our thoughts. These come from our perceptions and indoctrination from the moment we are born. How do we perceive the world? How do we react to life's circumstances? Where do our thoughts come from?

We perceive life with the eyes and thoughts and feelings that we have experienced from birth. Our indoctrination initially comes from our family environment, community, religious upbringing, culture, race, gender and nation. Our perceptions change as we grow up, we experience life outside our home, our parents, our school, our college and then, in the wider world, we are influenced by our working life, relationships and so on.

There are four levels of Perception:

- The physical (related to our Root & Sacral Chakras)
- The mind & the emotional (related to our Solar Plexus and Throat Chakras)
- The soul (related to our Heart Chakra and also the Eighth Chakra above the Crown)
- The spirit (related to our Brow & Crown Chakra and the Ninth Chakra above the Eighth)

It is helpful to remember that most people will perceive according to a combination of these chakras, but for many, the higher chakras will be latent. For the purpose of clarifying the nature of each chakra, I set them out individually below.

## **The Physical (related to our Root & Sacral Chakras)**

As humans we rely on our senses and perceptions, to give us a picture of ourselves and the world in which we live. This is our material level, our physical. These chakras relate to our fears, our sensations, our need to survive. The reality of this perception is mostly materialistic. We experience things that are there, things that we can see, touch and smell. Our reactions are usually instinctual. We see things exactly as they appear to be. If we were operating exclusively from these chakras, our will to survive dominates and our reactions will tend to be from fear or anger, or both. We react from sensations, based on our perceptions of life.

When we see problems from this perception, we react from a very basic human level. We come up with physical solutions to physical problems. At this level we are operating totally instinctively. In other words, we are aware of little more than our physical bodies, but we are not cognizant of our mental, creative and spiritual selves. In this state we are only aware of the obvious, remaining blind to our feelings and those of others. We are lacking any complex thinking, and simply act and react.

We need to be in the physical, to act and perform our everyday needs. This of course is helpful in dealing with life in a practical way addressing the needs and necessities of life (paying bills, doing shopping, caring for ourselves and our families). We just do what needs to be done without worrying our heads into thinking any deeper or analysing life. Sometimes we meet people who like to be very intense about life and this can be annoying and wearisome.

Instincts at this level can be very helpful because they can alert us to dangers before we actually perceive them. Therefore, this level of perception is vital and essential. We have to be effective in the physical world and take care of life in a practical way. But it can also be selfish, because we tend to be only concerned about our own survival and we may not always be considerate of other people's feelings.

Much of humanity has lived at this level for thousands of year and lifetimes. These chakras are of course pure and good in themselves, but they lack the wisdom of the higher chakras. Religious indoctrination comes from this level. This is the perception that all others are wrong or evil and need to be eliminated This is the level of 'an eye for an eye', 'a tooth for a tooth' perception.

## **The Mind & Emotional Perception (related to our Solar Plexus & Throat chakras)**

At this level, it is the mind that deduces our reality. This is the realm of beliefs, ideas and emotions because this type of perception can suddenly change and transform situations, causing them to be seen in a new light. For example, a single insight or flash of understanding, can instantly break us free from our negative thinking or feeling. Once we understand that our perception of that reality was based on our old way of thinking or feeling (in other words our indoctrination), we can change in that moment.

At this level the instincts are different from those of the physical, which is only concerned with survival and self-preservation. At this level, our perception is curious and inquisitive. We love to form and express ideas, beliefs and feelings. We can rise above the literal and see a wider range of possibilities.

If someone acted badly, or irrationally (to our perception), we actually think 'What has caused him/her to do that'. At this level we can perceive more than the physical, therefore we can come up with resolutions. We don't just simply disparage another, we realise that there must be something more happening behind the scenes.

Because we are not coming from fear or anger, we are able to start expressing our feelings, and ideas and because we have more possibilities, we are able to make effective changes and solve more complex issues. We can be more creative in our thinking, in our lives. We can truly change our perception of life and of ourselves, and of others.

This level of perception could also be very dangerous as it could keep us imprisoned unless we are willing to accept that, what we deem as our reality, is only a concept based on our past indoctrination.

If we allow our instincts for survival and self-preservation (chakras one and two) to dominate, without a willingness to see things differently, to accept others who may also have good instincts and good ideas, (chakras 3 and above) this is what can make us fanatics and extremists and this is where the danger lies.

## **The Soul (related to our Heart & Eighth Chakra)**

This is the level of the Soul. It is the realm where the Soul can experience itself through its journey through the chakras and initiations. At this level it is the Soul that guides, directs and encourages us to go from one lifetime to another, learning lessons, accumulating knowledge, bringing the unconscious to the conscious. All the time it understands it is on a sacred and epic journey and trusts the impulse that guides it.

At this level we find solutions to problems that the physical couldn't solve. We flow with the ebb and flow of the tide in a calmer and peaceful state. Everything we do, say or feel is coming from a higher perspective. We see the goal-post, not the ploughed fields. Life is then an expression of the sacred.

At this level, we know that we are all on a journey to grow, to heal the past, to understand ourselves at a deeper level, and to understand and appreciate others on the path with us. We see things differently. We are less judgmental. We are more considerate. We are more caring.

Our Soul perception enables us to have that confidence, that understanding that where we are at this moment, is exactly right for our soul's unfoldment and development.

## The Spiritual (related to our Brow & Crown and Ninth Chakra)

The Eagle is the bird with the wider vision as it soars well above other birds over valleys and mountains and can take in everything from the highest level possible. But it is also able to spot something very small a couple of thousand feet below. Eagle has the ability to see the entire picture or only a bit of it. This is the quality of the level of Spirit.

At this level of Spirit, we do not see ourselves as disconnected from the planet or from loved ones. There are no boundaries as our Soul has done its work of guiding us through the many experiences and once, we have reached the 4th Initiation, the Soul is no longer necessary. We are purely Spirit. At this level we recognise our Oneness. We are truly at One with all life.

We look at life totally differently. There is no separation from the Divine and the Physical. All is one. We do not see any life being separate from any other life.

Whenever we have a problem, it is helpful to try to rise up to the level of the Eagle and see the bigger picture. At this height the solution will simply come.

At the lower levels of perception, we need to find solutions to problems. However, at the highest level we simply flow with the essence of the Spirit within and things will just work out.

***Our perception of the world defines its very nature. We can vision the world into being beautiful, peaceful and loving. It always comes down to our perception of life and how willing we are to change it.***

As awakening comes, the awareness that there is something greater than the outer self begins to assert itself. Gradually our soul begins to make its presence felt and we no longer react from our emotions or thoughts. Our personality is very necessary for our growth. It is by going through every challenge, every experience, that we develop and unfold. Our personality, encompassing both the emotional and mental bodies, has to find a point of balance between them. Only then can we truly allow the Spirit within to guide our lives. We need to bring spirituality down into matter so that matter is transmuted by the light within.

Our Personality is vital to our growth. This changes every lifetime of course, depending on the circumstances into which our Soul chooses to incarnate. Our Soul knows which lessons still need to be learned and chooses the circumstances that will give us the best opportunities for learning those lessons which are so important to our growth.

**CHAPTER 2**

# The Soul, The Bridge, The Antahkarana

The Soul is a consciousness. It has the pure essence of Spirit within Itself, but the Spirit needs to experience itself and this is done through the vehicle of the Soul. The Soul has no form, it is a consciousness; therefore, it needs a form, a vehicle which is the human body, in order to evolve and grow. The journey of the Soul takes many lifetimes. As Souls, we have evolved and grown through Ages, Cycles, Rounds of Earth, Planetary Systems, Solar Systems. We continue until we reach that pinnacle of development - the full consciousness of Spirit, also known as the Christ Consciousness. Here I speak of the Universal Christ Light, not any individual being.

This means that we truly have as much time as we need to know ourselves, a time to assimilate the experiences that we face each lifetime. Every experience, whether good or bad, has a purpose – a lesson learned at a deeper level of understanding. But are these lessons, these experiences purely personal or are we something far greater than we give ourselves credit for. The knowledge that we could be more than the outer personality is both exciting and scary. So what are we?

The Soul is three-fold in nature. It is self-conscious (Personality); it is group conscious (Soul) and it is God-conscious (Spirit). The Soul has no personal or individual desires, neither does it have ambition. The Soul exists as a consciousness and is there to guide the personality (the human self) through multiple experiences. The purpose of life is about the personality, the individual person realising that there is more to life than just the physical and unfolding the spiritual qualities which lie inherent. Over many lifetimes the Soul guides and leads the personality forward until it reaches a stage when it becomes aware that there is something greater than the physical. This is the Journey through the chakras.

When this happens, the Soul slowly begins to assert its authority over the Personality, and it lifts its awareness to acknowledge that it is part of a group soul. It begins to work with the group soul, acknowledging the companions of old who are there in spirit to help and guide it forward. Slowly, the awareness widens beyond the Soul to the Spirit, and yet again wider still beyond the Spirit to the greater Cosmos. This is our God-conscious state.

In Chapter 10, I describe what the Spirit is, but here I want to talk about the Soul. The Soul is our conscience, that part of us which knows our path, knows what lessons we need to learn in order to continue to evolve and unfold our spiritual qualities. This is usually the part that we so often ignore because we are not listening. The part which fear keeps imprisoned. Our Soul is the force that guides us even though we may not be aware of the difference between the Soul and the personality.

When we are focused on our personality, it is the mental body and the emotions that rule us. These are both very strong forces within and like to keep us imprisoned, to control us. When the Soul begins to assert itself, neither the mind nor the emotions are happy because they know they will start losing control over us. We need to remember that at the Soul level we have free will. We cannot overrule the personality until the personality is ready to let go.

The journey of the Soul takes it through the experiences denoted by the chakras, all the time working with the influences of the Major Rays and then it meets its initiations with the lessons learned from these experiences. The soul lessons learned from its journey through the signs of the zodiac, enables the Soul to grow and unfold its petals. The Soul is like a Lotus flower, with many petals which will unfold slowly as the lessons are learned. It is said that when it is fully open, the lotus flower unfolds a thousand petals.

The question arises, how does the Soul assert itself? How can we know whether it is the Soul prompting us or our minds? How can we tell the difference between Soul and personality?

In the consciousness of the personality we are still trying to solve problems on the physical level. When we reach the understanding of Soul level, we flow with the ebb and flow of the tide, trusting that the solution will come from a higher perspective. We see the goal-post, not the ploughed fields.

The answer lies in knowing ourselves. By this I mean really knowing ourselves. When we are able to stand aside and observe our actions and reactions, thoughts and emotions. When we can do this dispassionately and accept what is happening without getting into anxiety, frustration, anger or fear, then we know that a lesson has been learned and this is our Soul understanding.

Earlier in this book I suggested working with and understanding the three E's (Experiment, Experience, Expression). There are also three other wonderful spiritual qualities to work with. These are:

- Detachment
- Discrimination
- Discernment

When we are faced with a situation that is challenging and possibly confrontational, it is helpful if we try pausing for a moment. Let's pause and stand still before reacting. By this gesture, this pause, we have gone within and allowed the Soul, the inner us, to take command. Then, when we do act, it will be from a more balanced and rational state (and more caring manner) rather than reacting immediately from our emotions or mind.

## **The Antahkarana – the Bridge**

Each time we reach a stage where we are raising our consciousness, our inner knowing, this is when we cross a Bridge. This is called the Antahkarana. It happens when the Soul has reached a new level of understanding, then we are ready to move forward, to another level.

There will come a point, after the 4th Initiation (Chapter 5) when there will no longer be a need for the Soul, as it will have done its work guiding the personality forward to its highest conclusion. Then we shall be pure Spirit.

CHAPTER 3

# Explanation of the Chakras or Centres In The Body

Chakras or Centres in the body are ports of entry of the Cosmic rays and life-force into the etheric body. They are also known as energy centres. There are seven major chakras in the body, 21 minor ones and 49 lesser ones. In this book I will deal with the seven major ones. Each chakra has seven different levels. I will share my understanding of each level.

The chakras are the vehicle through which the Soul learns and develops along the Path. Each chakra has soul lessons to teach us. The Chakras are linked to the Seven Major Rays of Creation and also to the Great Initiations that every soul has to go through along its Path. As we develop and unfold our spiritual qualities through each of the chakras, so does our consciousness expand. Chakras are sometimes known as 'the windows of the soul'.

Each chakra has a little disc which spins along the spine according to the Soul's development. As we evolve our chakras, this disc spins brighter and faster. A Master and Spiritual Teacher can tell the evolutionary path of a particular soul by looking at the spinning discs of the Soul's Chakras.

If any of our Chakras look dull and spin slowly, then that would suggest a blockage and that something is not functioning properly. Therefore, the vital force cannot enter and nourish the body. These blockages cause disease and disharmony in the parts of the body linked to that particular chakra. Blocked energy in our seven chakras can often lead to illness, so it's useful and important to understand what each chakra represents and what we can do to keep this energy flowing freely. The degree of development of these chakras determines how much of our Soul, Spirit can manifest through the personality.

## **The Seven Major Chakras are:**

| | |
|---|---|
| First Chakra | - Root (base of spine – Adrenals) |
| Second Chakra | - Sacral (sexual, generative centre, abdomen – Gonads) |
| Third Chakra | - Solar Plexus (around the stomach centre – Pancreas) |
| Fourth Chakra | - Heart Centre (balance of lower and upper chakras – Thymus glands) |
| Fifth Chakra | - Throat Chakra (Expression – Thyroid glands) |
| Sixth Chakra | - Brow (Third Eye – Ajna centre - Pituitary) |
| Seventh Chakra | - Crown Centre (Higher consciousness - Pineal) |

The three lower chakras relate to the personality and the instinctive life processes of the physical body. The fourth is the balance between the lower and upper chakras.

The three higher chakras relate to the higher consciousness – our higher perception and expression of the spiritual life.

The Crown Chakra is the last to become fully developed and functioning, bringing illumination of consciousness and full understanding of our spiritual self.

Each chakra has seven different levels, ie, in each chakra there is the level of the Root, Sacral, Solar Plexus, Heart, Throat, Brow and Crown.

The journey through the chakras offers us the opportunity to learn vital soul lessons.

The seven chakras are aligned thus:

> The Base of Spine to the Crown & Brow Chakra
> The Sacral Chakra to the Throat Chakra
> The Solar Plexus to the Heart Chakra

This may clarify why the Major Rays and the Initiations influence more than one chakra.

There are two other Chakras above the Crown (7th). These are:

> The Eighth which is related to our Soul and
> The Ninth which is related to Spirit.

See Diagram at the front of this book which shows the link between the chakras, rays, planets and colours.

# CHAPTER 4

# Explanation of the Seven Major Rays

From theosophical writings we understand that in very simplistic terms a Ray is an energy, a force, that was breathed from the Absolute Being. It is the energy that sustains the universal cosmic life. It is the driving force behind what makes us tick. There are seven major Rays of Creation. There are also minor ones. Each is distinct and yet inter-related to each other. Understanding the Rays help us to understand ourselves and those around us. Each Ray has seven sub-Rays.

The seven major Rays are a dynamic force in the Universe. We react to those forces and as the soul progresses on its journey we learn to cooperate with them and become masters of our destiny rather than just be driven by forces over which we have no control. The Rays embody the Divine Purpose and create the forms through which the divine idea can be manifested.

Every Ray is an expression of a greater life. The Rays are necessary for soul growth and development. The influence of the Rays is universal. They work through our chakras to help us unfold and develop spiritually. Souls can be influenced and be developing on two or three Rays in one incarnation.

We know that a solar system is composed of a sun with planets revolving around it in its sphere of attraction. We learn from the Ageless Wisdom that a constellation is formed of two or more solar systems held together by mutual attraction between their suns. The constellation to which our solar system belongs is composed of seven solar systems.

The Absolute Being created Seven Breath or Rays. These are seven differentiations of intelligent creative energy, which colour and express all creation as it exists within our constellation.

There is One Life, one Creator. This Being is One but reveals itself as Three, the primary Three which manifest the essence of the Creator. The One and the Three are acknowledged in many spiritual traditions. For instance in Christianity, we talk about Unity and Trinity (Father, Son and Holy Spirit). In the Hindu tradition, there is One and then the three: Brahma, Vishnu, Shiva. Again, there is Threeness in the terms Spirit, Soul and Body and Father, Mother, Child. One force, One Energy, which expresses itself primarily through Seven basic Qualities or Aspects.

It is said that when the Absolute Being breathed the first three Breaths the sacred Word was spoken. The sacred Word again is not as we recognise it, as a word, but rather the sound of the AUM, which is also a vibration of the first three major Rays:

| **A** | The First Ray of Will & Power was breathed forth |
| **U** | The Second Ray of Love & Wisdom was breathed forth |
| **M** | The Third Ray of Active Intelligence & Adaptability was breathed forth |

This was the first sound of Creation.

The life, the essence of the Absolute Being was expressed as white spiritual light. It divided this great Ray of Light into three to manifest its essence. These are the three Major Rays of Will & Power, Love and Wisdom and Active Intelligence and Adaptability. These three Major Rays embody the three principal facts of the creative consciousness of the deity, the Absolute Being.

**Ray 1** embodies the dynamic **Idea** of the Creator

**Ray 2** formulates the **Plan** upon which the form must be constructed, and the idea materialized/manifested

**Ray 3** organises the **Idea and the Plan** and puts it into form. This formation will eventually manifest the Idea and Purpose of the Creator.

Each Ray has a Logoi or Spirit ensouling it. One of these is the Logos of our own solar system, our own Divine God. These Seven Breaths or Rays are divided yet again into another seven, giving us the seven ages of man.

The seven Rays are the sum total of the divine Consciousness, of the Universal Mind.

The specific Ray upon which we are progressing in this cycle is not necessarily that of the Ray under which we were created. The soul travels along a certain Ray for a certain period or cycles, and during that cycle, according to the development of the higher bodies or vehicles, comes under other influences and vibrations. And any one individual is likely to be affected by two or more Rays during any given incarnation. There is a Soul Ray and there is a Personality Ray.

It is important not to 'pigeon-hole' the Rays in any way and especially people to Rays. The Rays operate on many different levels.

As human beings we evolve through our own self-expression and self-realization.

As we understand it, the Rays affect all the Kingdoms of nature, thus:

| | | |
|---|---|---|
| Humanity | (4th Kingdom) | is on 5th Ray - Concrete Knowledge & Science |
| Animal | (3rd Kingdom) | is on 6th Ray - Devotion |
| Vegetable | (2nd Kingdom) | is on 4th Ray - Harmony, Beauty, Balance |

Mineral        (1st Kingdom) is on 7th Ray - Organization and Ritual

In my first book, *Stepping Stones on the Spiritual Path*', I give more explanation on the Rays. The following is an excerpt:

*'The Seven Rays affect everything about who we are. There is a resonance with the chakras, the centres in the body, there is a resonance with colour, there is a resonance with the different planets. Every Ray represents an aspect of the Divine, emerging from Unity into creation where it is expressed. Each has a subjective aspect as well as an objective one. Each is a stable pure Essence which cannot be changed, but in the human realm the expression of each can be perverted through the mis-use of our freewill.......the Soul can work on one particular Ray for a very long time but this is not altogether exclusive as it will also function and experience other Rays. Eventually of course all the experiences will blend into one. This is the Christ Light, the White Light that is often spoken about.'*

# Definition of the Rays as described in theosophical writings:

The seven rays may be divided into two groups. The absolute major rays are 1, 2 and 3.

1) **Will & Power – The Will to Initiate**
This is the Ray with the dynamic idea, a powerful energy, the life-force. This is the Ray that initiates all that exists, the Ray of creation, power, activity. This is the essence of spirit; it can be divisive and destructive. It is also the Ray of Purpose, Creative Will. The driving sense of purpose is to create. It creates and then destroys in order to create. The Absolute Being breathed forth and creation was initiated. This is the Ray that holds the Logoic Principle and Intention. This is the lawgiver, the ruler. It is the manifestation of the divine masculine, active principle throughout the universe. From the place of separation, it is that undeniable inner Will to find and create a higher level of harmony both within ourselves and between all sentient beings. It causes us to challenge and break apart the status quo which may be holding us in a lower level of realization. The 1st Ray inspires life's motivational leaders.

2) **Love & Wisdom – The Will to Unify**
This is the Ray that unifies, carries out the Plan, gives form to life, thereby giving energy to the original principle and intention. It is a passive ray and embodies the Soul. It is a Ray that nurtures. It is an altruistic Ray. Those who vibrate to this Ray are people working under the influence of love. This Ray denotes surrendering, unconditional Love. It also initiates the impulse of unconditional love for life. It is the manifestation of the divine feminine principle of surrendered acceptance throughout the universe. It softens the destructiveness with passiveness and nurturing and with caring. It is the Mother concept, passive and nurturing. This Ray empathizes with the needs of humanity and expresses a pure compassion that willingly embraces life without judgement or the need to change the inherent imperfection in all sentient life and situations. The 2nd ray strongly inspires the selfless servants of life.

### 3) Active Intelligence & Adaptability – The Will to Evolve

This is the Ray of Philosophy, the ray of the thinker. It embodies the Idea and the Plan of 1) and 2) and puts them into action through the second group of rays in an active and intelligent way. This Ray harnesses and processes higher abstract wisdom delivering it in a form to provide a clear interpretation of our current, authentic reality. In other words, it's how we know what is real. People with a strong Ray 3 influence notice the natural patterning in life bringing the formless into form in such a way that can be understood and appreciated by many. The 3rd Ray inspires life's translators, creative artists and mathematicians.

## The second group of rays:

### 4) Harmony through Conflict – the Will to Harmonise

This is the Ray that is very prominent and influencing Humanity right now. Look around the world and see how much conflict there is and how we need to restore harmony and balance. But first we need to find harmony and balance within ourselves. This is the Ray that brings us the opportunity to attain harmony and balance through conflict, that is, through the depths of human experience. A very sensitive Ray that needs to dig deep to the roots to clear and cleanse. It can easily be pulled one way or another. Very artistic. Humanity needs to recognize its duality – Soul and personality. This Ray can bring peace through the conflict of human experiences. It is the Ray that teaches the art of living. Ray 4 is the divine rationalizing energy which helps us find right resolution with our environment and other sentient life. It is the Ray impulse which blends passion with compassion. It provides the discernment to confront unjust situations in a non-judgmental way. Its purpose is to break apart the lower harmony to find a more equitable higher one. People with highly active Ray 4 tend to be life's diplomats, politicians and teachers.

### 5) Concrete Knowledge & Science – The Will to Action

This is the Ray that says, '*I hear what you are saying but I need to realize it for myself.*' This is what is meant by concrete knowledge – we have to know it within ourselves. This is the Ray that likes to get right to the very cause and to work things out precisely and scientifically. This is a very mental ray and is happiest when it is getting down to the grit of the matter. It can be very analytical and searches for truth in a practical and scientific way. When we have realized something within, we just *know* this is our Truth and will approach spirituality in a very concretized way. This Ray loves knowledge but is careful that it is truth and not airy-fairy. It also facilitates the acquisition of right knowledge. The 5th Ray enables us to hold the infinite complexities of the universe as pure knowing within our beingness. This 'science' is abstract, all-encompassing and rather than realized, is more sensed, as an art form, like poetry in perpetual motion. This Ray enables us to attune to the universal flow and harness it for co-creative exploration, deeper understanding and further evolution. The 5th Ray animates life's scientists and creative business leaders.

6) **Idealism, Devotional & Inspirational – The Will to Cause**
This is a Ray that can be devoted to a cause, an ideal, or to an individual. This is the Ray of the Mystic. The Ray that has greatly influenced the Piscean Age. Very idealistic, very devotional and at times fanatical. It loves to bring the ideal into manifestation but can also be very one-pointed, fanatical, bigoted, intolerant and sometimes cruel in how it sets about to achieve its ideal. It is a Ray that can attain great faith which when rightly used can bring strong ethical attitudes into manifestation. The 6th Ray inspires us to stay continually focused on our life's purpose: to realise, unfold and express who we really are. It generates commitment and devotion to our cause, radiating our soul in all its brilliant colour. Ray 6 provides the unquenchable driving force to express our innate qualities and inspire others to shine their inner light too. Humanity's philosophers, spiritual leaders and performing artists are all driven by this ray's influence. The Ray that yearns for self-expression. As this Ray is receding, we are currently seeing its energies being perverted into fanatical extremist tendencies manifesting around the world, in various forms. But the positive aspect of this Ray is its quality of deep devotion and altruism.

7) **Law & Order, Ceremonial Ritual – The Will to Express**
This is the Ray that is influencing the Aquarian Age. This is the Ray of law and order, of organization and ritual. It shapes synchronistic order. The ritual can be both exoteric and esoteric. This is the Ray that expresses the

life-force through matter. It is the Ray that understands divine Law and the ability to understand and control the elements within one's own being. This is the Ray of the practical Mystic. It is concerned with putting into action the laws of the universe in a systematic and practical way. It is also known as the Ray of Beauty as it brings into operation those powers which are intensified by beauty and draws to itself the great Devas which are present at ceremonies. It is also the Ray of magic. Rituals are being played out around us constantly. Think of the rhythm and ritual of nature, and how nature interacts with the elements and plays out its rituals season after season. There is also the law and order within us. The spiritual law which is the great taskmaster and does not allow the soul to break the Law of Karma – if we do, then there are consequences. If we can master our inner distortions and pause just long enough in the drama of life, then we can open up to our inner guidance for the maximum benefit and upliftment of all. In this way, Ray 7 inspires life's magicians' and entrepreneurs.

# CHAPTER 5

# Explanation of the Initiations

'Initiation' quite simply means an expansion of consciousness During the course of many lives we go through a series of initiations which will finally free us from the continuous round of earthly incarnations. To understand what an initiation is we need to consider what the journey of the soul is and what exactly is the nature of its incarnation. When a soul comes down into incarnation, it has to go through the experiences of three of its layers, i.e. the personality, the first three chakras, and then proceed up towards the higher chakras, Soul and Spirit.

Initiations take place at Soul level, not at the physical. It is experienced by the soul at its own level. Each initiation means that the soul has gained mastery over one of the subtler bodies. Initiations are taken over many lifetimes and are truly a slow process. Initiations are a valuable and essential phase of our spiritual evolution. Each initiation marks an achievement; it indicates the soul has attained greater direction over the personality through which it is trying to express itself.

Initiations are also an opportunity for new beginnings as the soul is then ready for a new level of consciousness. Initiations may work over a number of chakras at the same time.

There are four very important initiations related to the four elements, i.e. Water, Air, Fire and Earth. There are also nine individual soul Initiations that we experience in the course of our journey through the chakras, although these are also related to the elements. Every experience we go through forms a part of one or other of these major initiations by which we eventually gain mastery over ourselves, mastery over the circumstances of our lives, and mastery over the very substance of matter itself. We prepare and experience different degrees of initiations at the same time, although we may not have completed any one of them.

Throughout the history of humanity, there have been examples of lives that have exemplified the life of every Soul. One of these was the life of the Master Jesus. His life demonstrated the path of every soul and indeed the initiations he went through, culminating in the great initiation of the crucifixion and resurrection, (the 4th Initiation) marked him out as a true master.

I have explored the four major Initiations of the Elements related to the subtler bodies of the personality and these are:

**WATER:** Waters signifies the 'psyche', the soul of man. It is symbolic of the emotional nature of man. The waters of the soul, reflecting our emotions can be like the see-saw, up one minute and down the next. In other words, we can be tranquil and still or tempestuous and unsettled. Our emotions need to be brought under the control of the Master Soul. Before the soul can advance on the path of initiation, the Light consciousness within must discipline that soul and make it peaceful enough to reflect the true image of the higher consciousness.

The Water Initiation is like a baptism. We are refreshed and cleansed by the Water Initiation and it means that we are no longer at the mercy of our strong, negative emotions. The Soul has learned how to remain tranquil and calm as it meets its challenges. The Soul has now reached a level of tranquillity where it no longer reacts and judges. It has conquered its fears and anxieties. It becomes like a calm sea shining and reflecting the higher worlds in the waters of the soul.

Baptism is also about cleansing and purification. As the soul learns to conquer its stormy emotions, it learns how to live peacefully, and this tranquillity will then manifest in the physical body enabling the Soul to live a healthier life.

Undisciplined and uncontrolled emotions disturb the bloodstream and glandular system.

**AIR:** The Air element is symbolic of the mind. The human mind is as difficult to understand and conquer as the emotions. The 'monkey' or lower mind can obstruct the development and progress of the Soul, but ideally, it works with the heart to illuminate and guide us. Dispassion is one of the most difficult lessons for the soul to learn. It is so very easy to get upset emotionally.

The purpose of the Air initiation is to allow the higher mind to take control and become the ruler of our thoughts. In other words, we need to purify our thinking so that we can receive spiritual truths and when our thoughts are purified, there will no longer be a clash between the mind of the personality (the earthly mind) and the Higher Mind, which holds our consciousness. The earthly mind of the personality does all it can to confuse us because it is afraid to lose its grip or control over us.

The Air Initiation brings recognition and discrimination between the two minds of man – the earthly mind and the mind of Christ, the Higher or Heavenly Mind.

If we allow the Higher Mind to deal with life's problems, the soul will take on the qualities of Christ consciousness. It will absorb these spiritual qualities and live its life in accord to all that is true and beautiful.

The Air Initiation teaches us how to be of service to others. Through the process of Initiation, the Higher Mind, the Light within, empowers the soul to serve out of pure love.

**FIRE:** It is the Fire Initiation which enables the Soul to appreciate the Light and Love in its life. The Soul undergoes a series of degrees in order to develop that divine consciousness. Fire is Love and this Initiation brings the Soul that warmth, that loving consideration for life itself. Love can be active on all planes. When we are still operating from the lower chakras and in the process of undergoing the Water and Air Initiations, the Soul becomes aware of love as a passion that burns and consumes but as we proceed on the path we are then able to create and give life on the highest plane.

When the soul passes the Fire Initiation it undergoes a unique and special experience which will change its whole life.

**EARTH**: After going through the first three Initiations of Water, Air and Fire, the Soul still needs to learn how to control physical matter in a wise and loving way. In other words, all that it has experienced through the previous Initiations, it needs to put into practice and thus this Initiation is often likened to a Crucifixion, a surrender of the Soul to the Highest, the Spirit. Every Soul needs to go through a form of crucifixion, whether this is through the Emotional, Mental or Physical. It reaches a stage when it has developed and unfolded its spiritual qualities to the highest degree; and it now needs to surrender to the highest within -the Spirit – the Christ Consciousness.

Our task, as Souls, is to master the four elements of our nature and continue our journey as Lightworkers.

*It needs to be understood that we cannot pigeon-hole either the Great Initiations or the Seven Major Rays that the Soul takes along the Path. The degree to which the Initiations and the Rays influence or affect the Chakras very much depends on the Soul's understanding and learning of its lessons. The explanations and the links which I have given in this book are only a brief and maybe a clumsy interpretation of how the chakras are linked to the major Rays and Initiations. It needs to also be remembered that within each Ray there are seven sub-Rays.*

The following are the initiations of each individual on the journey of the soul.

# 1st Initiation– the Birth of the Spirit Within

This is the birth of the Christ Spirit in the heart. This is influenced by the 7th Ray of Ceremonial Law & Order, which conditions and governs the energies of this Initiation. It influences the 1st Chakra – The Root – and embodies **The Will to Live and Survive.** At the birth, the channel (the Bridge) between the personality and the Soul (the Antahkarana) begins to open. This Initiation is about understanding primal fear and the will to survive.

This is about the physical appetites and the demands of the body; gaining mastery over our physical appetites, survival and the instinctive will to survive. The flesh and the body begin to be obedient; the soul begins to gain a bit of mastery here. We learn by experience – we don't just go and beat somebody up or go to other extremes just because we have an 'urge'. We are beginning to understand our own appetites but also, we are becoming more aware of the needs of the group as well as our own.

This is about the lesson of the Water Element, which affects our emotions and our psyche, not the deep emotions of the solar plexus but the sensations and our instinct to survive. These are feelings but on a much lower level and this is what we need to master. This Initiation and the 2nd take place on the astral level. The 1st Initiation is as simple as that – mastering lower level appetites of the flesh. It means that we learn not to give way to our appetites and passions in the sense of 'I want, and I will have.' Instead we say 'I want but I have to be conscious of the group.' It's a huge learning curve here because the heart and the mind haven't developed properly yet. At this level, we can't reason things out nor can we show compassion because we haven't yet developed the love of the heart.

With the 1st Initiation we begin to realize 'I can't have it because I've got to be aware of my responsibility to the others, clan, tribe, group, family etc. Others need it too'. That instinctive need is there but there is also an understanding of how it is going to affect others.

## 2nd Initiation - The Baptism

The 2nd Initiation is a very difficult one and some of humanity are experiencing this right now – mastering the emotional sensations within ourselves. The 2nd Initiation is so vital because humanity needs to learn to master its emotions. We can see now in humanity how the emotions are probably the most difficult to control. It's not about suppressing these sensations, rejecting them or ignoring them, it's about elevating them. We begin to understand that wanting and doing these negative things is just not right. The soul can think 'Oh my goodness that was a terrible thing I said.' The understanding is there, that comes from the heart but when we're living in that 2nd Chakra and possibly in a toxic atmosphere where everything is heightened it's very challenging. That's why the 2nd Initiation is known to be the most difficult and the most painful Initiation because humanity has struggled for hundreds of lifetimes to get through that.

In the 1st Initiation we begin to accept our instinct - that we are more than just individuals within a community whereas the 2nd Initiation builds on this giving us a wider vision of the Group Purpose and our Group Plan. We're living in a world surrounded by people, family, friends, community and nations enabling us to be aware that we are global citizens. That is the vision for the 2nd Initiation.

It is connected to the 2nd Chakra- the Sacral- and embodies **The Will to Feel.** As this Sacral Chakra is also linked to the Brow Chakra, we also have the influence of the 6th Ray of Devotion and Abstract Idealism. The Abstract Idealism shapes up the energies of this Initiation. It can also be fanatical. It's still the Water element and the Initiations take place at the astral level. We probably need to go through many lifetimes to bring the emotional body under the complete control of the soul.

## 3rd Initiation – The Transfiguration

This Initiation is also connected to the 5th Ray of Concrete Knowledge and Science. This Initiation takes place at the lower mental level. The 1st and 2nd Initiations take place at the Astral level, but the 3rd one takes place on the lower mental. The 3rd Initiation is again about another bridge of the Antakharana. It is connected to the 3rd Chakra- the Solar plexus – and embodies **The Will to Think.**

After the 2nd Initiation, the lower nature, the personality begins to lose its hold over the soul, therefore the desire to serve, to express love and to make progress in service becomes more powerful. The soul consciousness now begins to govern the activities of the personality. The soul begins to assert itself and to say 'hey- here I am! You've had your way and now it's my turn and let's all work together - it's all about Unity.'

At the 3rd Initiation the individual is transfigured into the Light of the Soul. We can often see people radiant with light and we can see this in their eyes. This is where the Soul starts to shine through because this is what the 3rd Initiation is about- Transfiguration. The entire personality, the lower self is bathed in the essence of the soul. This is the supreme secret which the 3rd Initiation reveals to the soul.

Sometimes, or even possibly all the time, the human mind can find the emotions difficult to handle. The mind has its thoughts and ideas, and often endless chatter, but emotions can be all over the place. All that is needed is something to happen and we react. Whilst the mind can say 'OK I can cope with this' the emotions can be very vulnerable and sensitive, feeling upset, hurt, angry. Until we learn to control those emotions, and this is the purpose of the 3rd Initiation- our reasoning mind will not submit to the mastery of the Soul.

## 4th Initiation – The Great Renunciation (the Crucifixion)

This is the Initiation that Jesus took as Jesus, and this is connected to the 4th Ray of Harmony through Conflict. It's also about Harmony and Beauty. This Ray is connected to the 4th chakra – The Heart- and embodies **The Will to Love (Unconditional Love).**

This Initiation takes place on the higher mental level. The 3rd was at the lower mental, the 4th is at the higher mental. During this Initiation or during the lifetime of the one that takes this Initiation the soul can go through great suffering because it is the Renunciation. It is possible that at this Initiation we may have to give up absolutely everything that is important to us. Jesus gave up his family, he gave up his mother and he just left to do his work. In essence we all have to do that in one lifetime or another. To give up the people we love, the home and conditions that we love; if money means a lot to us, we have to let go of that too. What we are actually giving up is the attachment. Some people have money, but they're not attached to it, others have money and they're very attached to it because it makes them feel secure.

This is why this Initiation is called the Renunciation because this is where we have to surrender the personality. We are literally surrendering the whole of the personality, all our feelings, all our emotions. This is at one with the Elders who gave back to God everything that they had attained. We then become pure Spirit. Often, we give up life itself which is what Jesus was prepared to do. Whether that happened or not doesn't matter, he was prepared to give his life and that's the Great Renunciation. This is the incredible bridge of Antakharana from the soul to the Spirit.

There will come a point when we will no longer need the Soul, and this is it. The personality has gone, the Soul releases its hold. Once the needs and desire of the personality (the ego) has gone, we don't need the Soul, we are now pure Spirit. This is what the 4$^{th}$ Initiation is about. When the Soul has progressed through all the Chakras, and reached this level of Initiation and understanding, it has mastered the personality and is ready to move on.

The Fire Initiation brings the warmth and the Light to that individual soul to uplift them to a higher consciousness. This is about letting go because that fire has consumed not just the personality but also the Soul.

At the level of this Initiation, we are no longer Souls, we are Spirit. It is a supreme Initiation. We have now joined the group of Master Souls.

## 5$^{th}$ Initiation – the Revelation

Through this Revelation we are aware of the Divine Will and Purpose of the Creator. This Initiation takes place at the Buddhic level. This is when the Seven Paths of the Higher Evolution are revealed in a cosmic vision. That's why it's called The Revelation. The entirety of the return journey to the prime Creator is revealed.

At this level of Initiation, the Master is taken off the Wheel of Rebirth; we do not have to keep coming back unless we wish to serve Earth. This is an all-consuming Initiation, where The Master becomes a Master of compassion, of love, of understanding. It's just enormous and we are talking about perfection, and liberation because the mind and the emotions aren't there. There's no karma either. It's purity and therefore the Initiate now becomes The Master of the Five Planes of Human Evolution.

In the Initiations $1^{st}$ – $4^{th}$ we have had God's love, we've been developing love, creative love etc. When we have gone through the $5^{th}$, $6^{th}$ and $7^{th}$ Initiations it's about the Will of God. Understanding the Will of God and after that it becomes the Purpose of God.

## 6$^{th}$ Initiation - The Decision

This Initiation takes place at the Atmic level (higher vibration and understanding- almost God. So many labels make definition here difficult). At this point the Initiate needs to choose one of the 7 Paths of Higher Evolution or to remain on the evolutionary planet that the Initiate is on. We have choices and this depends on which Path we choose to follow. Do we want to stay in the planetary scheme that includes Earth, or do we want to move on to the other Paths which involve other planets and universes? Therefore, this Initiation is called The Decision.

## 7$^{th}$ Initiation– The Resurrection

This Initiation takes place on the Monadic level. This is also known as the return of the Prodigal Son to the Father- a return to the original state of Being in the originating Source. This is the understanding about the force which animates all life on the planet. It is about the real understanding of what love is. Not our understanding of emotional love but what that word 'Love' really means to all life. It is not just on this planet, it's the whole solar system. Then we become a concentrated point of Light. So, at this level, we will become a fusion of a concentrated point of Light.

The following are the two other Initiations that we have understanding of after the Seventh.

## 8th Initiation – The Great Transition

This is where the nature and purpose of duality is revealed. We will then understand the underlying purpose for all the planetary activities and the two cosmic principles of polarity in this universe and the relationship between them and what that means.

## 9th Initiation – The Refusal

The information on the 9th Initiation that the Masters have given us in all the teachings that have come down to us from Madame Blavatsky, from the Master DK and other teachers is called the Refusal. The purpose of the Solar System is revealed and, as I understand it, the current Solar system is the second one in a series of three systems. We are talking solar systems not planetary.

The First Solar system was qualified by the 3rd Ray – the Mind of God, then we have the 2nd Solar system, qualified by the 2nd Ray, which is the Love of God and the 3rd Solar system would be qualified by the Purpose of God. The very nature of existence is revealed, and with that the realization of what Creation was really about, as well as the purpose of all the Planetary Logoi and the rest of the Galactic civilization- *(this sounds like Star Wars)*. We have now run out of words because language is so limited. The Refusal of the Initiation is the Refusal to stay behind. The Initiate cannot refuse – they have to move forward. When we've taken the 9th Initiation that's it – we've gone beyond, and we cannot refuse to stay behind. Whereas in the 4th, 5th, 6th Initiations we can choose to go forward, and/or we can choose to serve Earth but once we've taken this 9th Initiation we move forward on our cosmic journey and we don't look back.

CHAPTER 6

# Explanation of the Colours

Colours are very significant in that they all have special qualities as they relate to the soul lessons through the Chakras. Every colour has seven degrees of shade. As we unfold our chakras and learn our soul lessons these colours become more vibrant and shine more brilliantly. Each of the seven major chakras has a colour which vibrates to our development and unfoldment. One only has to look at a rainbow to see the magnificence of the colours of the spectrum.

In the following chapters where I describe the seven major chakras, I state the colour that relates to that chakra. Below I give a further explanation of the meaning and quality of each of the colours.

## **RED**

Red is one of the very powerful colours in the spectrum. It is our drive, our energy. It gives us vitality, stamina and is very forceful. It is a colour that motivates us to go forward. It can also be overwhelming and instinctively passionate. It is related to the Root Chakra and to the Will to Survive. This is a very active colour.

## **ORANGE**

Orange is another very powerful colour. In healing it can help to strengthen the immune system. It brings tremendous fire energy, thereby refreshing, stimulating and uplifting. This colour can help to lift depression and low mood. It is particularly helpful for a positive attitude of mind. It can be used to increase strength and vitality and acts rather like a tonic. This colour is related to the Sacral Chakra. An active colour.

## **YELLOW**

This is the colour of creativity, strength and power. It brings courage. It helps to inspire and motivate the Higher Consciousness. Through it we attain a more balanced and understanding attitude of mind. This colour helps us to balance our emotions and at the same time encourages us to develop and unfold our creativity. This is also a very uplifting colour for the soul. This colour is related to the Solar Plexus. Also a very active colour.

## **GREEN**

The colour of Green has the most wonderful qualities for cleansing and clearing. It is a colour that blends and balances. It is the colour of nature and we can see how nature blends all the different shades of green. We can see nature at work and how the rhythm of the seasons blends so beautifully. Green is the colour of Mother Earth. It is also worth bearing in mind that this is a colour which helps fertility. Mother Earth continually re-fertilizes herself. This colour is related to the Heart Chakra and as we unfold this Chakra, we bring harmony and balance to our Soul. It is both active and passive.

## **BLUE**

This colour is so very helpful to bring peace and tranquillity to the soul. It is a very calming colour and helps us to find that place of steadiness within ourselves, especially when we are experiencing tumultuous challenges. It is a colour that brings us that support, that constancy in our lives when the soul is reaching out for succour. This colour is related to the Throat Chakra. The colour blue helps us to express ourselves in a calm and steady manner. It is a very passive colour.

## INDIGO

This is the colour of dawning spiritual realization, of conscious contact with the heavenly spheres. It is the colour that enables us to see clearly, through perceptions, through conditioning. It is also a colour of mystery as it both hides and clarifies, when the Soul is ready for that higher realization. This colour is related to the Brow Chakra (the Third Eye) and helps us to see clearly, perceiving life from a higher octave.

## VIOLET

Violet is a very deep colour and symbolizes the spiritual understanding behind all life. This is also another colour of mystery. It helps the Soul to understand and penetrate deeper into the realms of the unknown. It is a colour of majesty, rituals and ceremonies. This colour helps us to reach heights of spiritual knowledge, particularly related to the Crown Chakra ***'I know that I Am'***.

## GOLD

The colour Gold is often associated with the Higher Consciousness and Enlightenment. It can bring illumination to the Soul. It is a majestic colour. A colour of joy. The colour of the Sun and we all feel better when the Sun is shining. It is a strong active colour which can bring courage to the Soul. A very uplifting colour.

## AMETHYST

The colour Amethyst is associated with the wisdom of the inner heart. It brings understanding to the Soul. It awakens the higher mind. It brings a very deep understanding of the inner mysteries to the Soul. It helps the Soul to reach a deeper level of knowing and understanding what it is experiencing.

**CHAPTER 7**

# The First Chakra is the Root – Our Foundation

This is the I AM at the basic level
It is the Will to Survive - rooted in FEAR

> **Influences & Links:**
>
> Colour is RED (see Chapter 6 for more explanation on the colours)
>
> Planet is Saturn
> Saturn is the planet which tests us. It holds the blue-print for each incarnation and takes us deep down into our foundation, our root so that we can learn and clear the dross.
>
> Element is Earth
> The Earth is our foundation. It is our Root. It also provides us with our nourishment. We need to be grounded on Earth so that we can bring down our Spiritual Higher Consciousness into matter. Learning the lessons of the first three initiations and bringing those realities back to earth and living it. In other words, living our Truth – walking our Talk!
>
> Soul Lesson is to overcome and rise above our fears
> This soul lesson is about understanding our foundation, our roots and grounding ourselves. We have many opportunities to face our fears, to understand our instinct for survival and to rise above and overcome. It teaches the Soul to survive, despite the pain, tribulations and challenges.
>
> Possible physical problems:
> Eating disorders/malnourishment; Adrenal insufficiency; problems with feet, legs or coccyx; spinal problems; immune-related disorders; osteoporosis or other bone disorders; haemorrhoids; constipation; prostate problems.

## **The First Chakra – Root - Adrenals**

The 1st chakra, known as the Root, is found at the very base of the spine, between the anus and the genitals and is influenced by the 1st Ray of Will and Power, the colour is red, and it is influenced by Saturn. Saturn is the energy, the force, the great tester, which will not let us pass through anything until the soul knows it has unfolded that chakra and learned that lesson to its fullest degree.

The Root chakra is primal energy, it's the energy of instinct, survival, self-preservation- it's the me, me, me first. Although that sounds selfish, in actual fact it's the very start of our journey and we have no concept at that point about selfishness or unselfishness because we haven't yet developed the heart centre or the mind. It is pure survival. Wherein the heart centre is about consideration of others, unselfishness and loving others, the root chakra is not there yet. The Root chakra is the very root of life, of the beginnings of everything. The main objective is survival and self-preservation; and of course, the 1st Ray of Will and Power is powerful, both destructive and creative because it is the Will energy, the Will to Survive, the Will to power.

This is the field of unconscious level. This is where our indoctrination, our habits, our belief systems, our perceptions are. Think of the beginnings of Man from the Root races (see description of Root Races in Glossary). These Races, as we know from Theosophical Teachings, began with the Polarian, then the Hyperborean, the Lemurian, the Atlantean and currently the Aryan. These races have evolved from other kingdoms of nature to animal type man and then to man. There was that instinct for survival because they were struggling with the elements and other kingdoms of nature all the time. In those days, there was nothing written to say, 'this is the way,' they had to go by their own instincts; there was nothing written that said 'you should do this, this is the way it's been done for thousands of years', they didn't have anything like that, so their instinct was, create – survive - destroy in order to survive, so therefore the Root chakra is a very powerful chakra and it needs to be fully unfolded and understood.

It is the chakra that gives us stability because we've got to create some balance; we need to be grounded and we've got to understand the Root chakra before we can move on. If we block the Root chakra, we're in trouble. Yes, we can develop the other chakras but only to a certain degree. However, if we haven't got that understanding, that stability, that grounding, then we have problems. The main point to remember is that we can use our instinct in a positive way, rising above the fears and overcoming them so that we can take that strength, that primal power and move upwards towards the other chakras.

This instinct activates the chakra, activates **US** as an individual Being. In other words, it starts the engine; before we are just a car sitting still going nowhere, but the Root chakra activates the engine. It gives us stimulation. All humanity has to go through the Root chakra and upwards towards the other Chakras, to attain the highest degree of consciousness at all levels. At this moment in time, the mass of humanity is supposed to be on the sacral and solar plexus. But that doesn't mean that we have totally learnt all the lessons of the Root. The Sacral affects the sex hormones. You only have to look around the world today to see how many predators there are, how much abuse there is, it means that these people have not fully developed all the different levels.

We start from the root, but we can also move on to the lessons of the following chakras even though the lesson of the first chakra has not been fully learned. This is because each chakra has seven different levels. Sometimes by going through a few of the chakras at a higher level, for example, the understanding heart, it can help us cope with some of the more difficult levels in the Root and the Sacral centres. The Root and the Sacral centres are probably the hardest for humanity to go through and these are connected to the 1st and 2nd Initiations. These are the hardest and the most difficult because we are dealing with primal instinct and primal energy and when I say primal, I mean animalistic.

From theosophical writings, we have the knowledge that Sanat Kumara, known as the Planetary Logos, came to earth 18 million years ago and brought the soul consciousness to humanity. Before that it was primal, animalistic so this was about early Lemurian times, which was animalistic in nature. It was only later when Sanat Kumara brought down the consciousness and the Path of Initiation into the soul, that 'ape man' began to evolve a consciousness.

Back in the 80's there were some people caught up in New Age things and wanting to raise their kundalini and forcing this. In my time as a healer I came across a number of them who had done this and had suffered consequently because their bodies were not ready for the huge force of energy that engulfed them. Some people thought that in order for them to become really enlightened they needed to raise their kundalini. That was dangerous because their bodies were not ready. The kundalini must not be forced. The Soul and the Spirit will know when the kundalini is ready to rise. The Root chakra is the fire of kundalini and we do need the kundalini **fire** to evolve but only when it's done in a natural, safe way and the soul knows when the time is right, and we are ready. It must not be forced. The Kundalini needs to rise in a natural way as we evolve. If allowed to happen naturally, there will be no mishaps, no problems physically, emotionally or mentally.

As said above each chakra has seven different levels. Therefore, that instinct in the 1st Chakra moves from the Root up to the Crown **within** the Root chakra. The Root chakra itself has the seven levels consisting of: Root, Sacral, Solar Plexus, Heart, Throat, Brow and Crown.

Let's now go through the different levels.

## **The root level of the Root chakra**

This is the Will to Survive; it's about power, the Will to Power and the Will to Survive. In a sense it's the I AM but at a basic level. The Will to Survive, the Will to Be, the Will to Live is the I AM. The I AM is the very essence of spirit unmanifested. It could be said that those souls who are still experiencing the lessons in the Root chakra are very strong-willed, because they've got that energy, they **will** get there because everything depends on that will to survive. These people will walk over anyone; flatten anything in their way if they get that instinct to survive. Even now you see people who are so determined to get their own way and they can also get very angry if they don't get it.

Above I've talked about the instinct and the will to survive. What's behind all these **is fear**; with the instinct to survive there is **fear**. There are many different types of fear. But this is primal fear which can be quite disturbing. It can get out of control because if we put somebody in a room with, for example, a rat or a spider, and they have a phobia about this, that person will scream and kick because the fear of survival is there, even if the object is a mouse or something very small. The primal fear is probably one of the worst fears we can have because it's survival 'I must live, come what may and anyone, anything or any circumstance that gets in my way I'm going to fight with everything I've got'. At this level we cannot reason with the mind because we haven't developed the mind.

## The sacral level in the Root chakra

This is the reproductive, creative, sexual stuff. At that basic level the sacral is going to be quite primal. Basic sex, in other words, carnal knowledge, affects the sexual organs etc at the sacral level and because we haven't yet developed the heart centre, we may not understand the responsibility to deal with these urges, these desires. The hormones are working but we don't really understand them. So, we give into them. We can misunderstand those desires at the sacral level, for example, ape man has an urge for ape woman and they just get on with it. All they understand is – I have an urge, a desire and that's it. This is how the sacral is affected. We start off with the primal fear and then we go on to experience the desires, the urges within.

## The solar plexus level in the Root chakra

We've had the primal fear and instincts, but these urges are something we cannot understand at a deeper level. All we understand is 'I want', 'I get' and if 'I don't get' – look out; fight; survival. It's very much 'this belongs to me'. We are responding to this urge and that's where the instinct is for fighting and getting. The solar plexus is the seat of our emotions. On a higher level those emotions can be beautiful; those feelings of joy, love, happiness and consideration, thoughtfulness for others and especially creativity. But at this level, the primal fear, the emotions would not be the beautiful ones. It would be survival again. If we cannot get what we want, we are upset, hurt, angry and possibly bitter and resentful.

There's this fear of not surviving and fear for the future because the emotions are involved. At this level emotions of fear and anger could be very prevalent. Although in the solar plexus we can have all the wonderful emotions of love, we can also have the opposite. We fear for the future because if we find ourselves in a situation where we feel less adequate, less capable than others, perhaps in a family, work, friends' situation, this instinctual fear can damage us to the core. We may also need to deal with feelings of inadequacy, low esteem, lack of confidence, feelings of being unloved. It may also provoke hatred and anger and jealousy, it overwhelms us and if it's primal, remember at this level there's no higher mind, there's no heart to balance, there's nothing there. It is as it is in front of us. This is moving even now from the Root to the Sacral to the Solar Plexus.

## The heart level in the Root chakra

It may have taken many lives to progress this far; maybe we have had many lives developing just the Root of the Root, we may have had many lives developing the Sacral of the Root and the Solar Plexus of the Root. However, when we get to the Heart level of this chakra something begins to stir, it's still primal but some higher feeling and understanding is beginning to stir. Remember, however, that beneath everything is still that instinctual fear, because fear and the will to survive is still the primal root. Therefore, as we develop at the heart centre level, we begin to realize other feelings but at the same time we could be bringing the fears with us. For example, we can have feelings for someone but then the fear comes in because we may think, 'something may happen, it won't last' because this could be coming from self-doubt, uncertainty. There's also a fear of being alone; the fear of commitment. If that soul, because it is still learning from the root, sacral and solar plexus, hasn't got the confidence which comes from the mind and heart, then the chances are they will go on primal instinct. So, there's fear and a lack of self-worth, self-esteem and confidence in oneself. This affects the heart. This can provoke feelings of sadness, depression. The lesson here is to go deeper into the understanding of the heart.

## The throat level in the Root chakra

The throat is the communication centre. This is where we have the opportunity to express our creativity, our feelings, our fears and if we cannot communicate, if we cannot voice who we are, what our feelings are, our thoughts for the future, we begin to doubt ourselves. Again, going back to self-worth, if we don't think highly enough of ourselves, we cannot express ourselves. Unless we are strong enough how can we communicate what our needs are? So far it is all emotions - we are still in our emotions whatever they may be, our heart is beginning to slightly understand a little – how can we communicate this? We can only do this through raising the consciousness because at that level we can only communicate primal instincts, primal fears and primal emotions. We may not have the words or the clarity and understanding and wouldn't really know what we're trying to say. We have an opening to the heart but not enough to give us that deep understanding, there's no wisdom there yet.

At this level, we're still in the basics; every day is what it is, there's no real ability to express ourselves or communicate properly at this level. We are still developing as human beings and here we need to remember too the group consciousness, we are developing as a human individual but also, we are part of a group. In those early days we lived in tribes or clans, and this is in our sub-conscious. We continue the group consciousness in this day and age but in different relationships, such as family, school, community, work, etc. It also depends whether the people around us are able to understand what we are trying to communicate because they're coming from their own perceptions. But it's the beginning of an opportunity for the future, perhaps there's a glimmer of 'I need to voice' whatever that may be ', I need to voice something'. So, we have come from the root, sacral, solar plexus and heart and the throat and then we come to:

## **The brow level in the Root chakra**

The Brow is the Third eye. It's how we perceive, how we see people, how we are conscious of the world around us. It is how we become more aware of our group, our family etc. How do we feel, how do we communicate with others – how do we see them? Do we feel a part of them, or do we feel totally isolated? Is it down to self-worth again, is it back to survival and how we socialize with people? Because with all these things we can go two ways with it, we can either be 'right I'm going to put my stamp down on this family/group' and we can be very, very aggressive and assertive, or we can suppress all that in instinctual survival ways ('let's not get involved' syndrome) but still harbour emotions of anger, hatred/envy, of bitterness and resentment and maybe we can't even voice that. We are perceiving only at the basic primal level. However, this is also the opportunity to see life more clearly.

## The crown level in the Root chakra

When we get to the Crown, we would normally think of this as enlightenment. When we speak of the Crown we think of the Buddha, the Master who has reached enlightenment. In a sense the Crown is associated or linked to spirituality - the higher consciousness. On the primal level - how do we attain or even understand spirituality? Our spirituality is there in essence. The essence of Spirit is there in all of us from the very beginnings from the Root to the Crown. The essence of Spirit is there from the very moment of Creation, so when you get to the Crown of the Root chakra the instincts can become 'there's more' but you have no idea what that is. This is because the essence of Spirit within is giving us that instinct and that's the I AM of that level. 'I know there's something more', 'I don't know what it is, 'but I know there is more' – that is INSTINCT at the highest positive level.

**Conclusion:** Understanding the different levels does help us to look at humanity and not just see the conflict and chaos, the pain and suffering but rather looking deeper as to why some people are going through such conflicting and challenging times. It helps us to understand why some people can kill with no compunction whatsoever, no conscience. There are those that can abuse and hurt others and yet there are also other people however tough and strong, they cannot hurt or kill. There are people in forms of life who can be totally ruthless and selfish - **they're** going to get what **they** want- survival - and they don't care how many people they trample over to do that. They are still evolving, just as we are. Humanity is evolving through crisis. This is very much the influence of the Fourth Ray, Harmony Through Conflict. We still have a long way to go as we work through the different levels of each Chakra, but we will get there. We need that faith and trust in the way that we are led. Trusting that our Soul will guide us towards that Pole-Star, culminating in that Christ-consciousness.

# The Second Chakra is the Sacral

**The Will to Feel - Desire**

> **Influences & Links:**
>
> <u>Colour is Orange</u> (see Chapter 6 for more explanation on the colour)
>
> <u>Planets are Moon and Mars</u>
> Mars is the planet which gives us energy, which drives us forward. It is fiery and powerful. The Moon is associated with this chakra through the water element. Represents the feminine, procreation and regeneration.
>
> <u>Element is Water</u>
> The water element symbolises our emotions and in this Chakra it is about overcoming negative desires which can threaten to overwhelm us and instead becoming more tranquil.
>
> <u>Soul Lesson</u>
> To understand and balance our desires and sensations. The lesson is also to bring us peace and tranquillity. To work with our passions in a positive way.
>
> <u>Possible physical problems</u>
> Bladder, spleen, pancreas, the uterus, ovaries. Also, sexual dysfunction, impotency, frigidity, fibroids, endometriosis, menstrual dysfunction, ovarian cysts or cancer. Plus conditions like diverticulitis, ulcerative colitis, Inflammatory bowel disease. Chronic low back pain or sciatica, appendicitis.

## The Second Chakra is The Sacral - Gonads

The Sacral Chakra, connected to the 2$^{nd}$ Ray of Love and Wisdom, is located just below the belly button and is about **the Will to Feel.** This chakra is about desire and sensation. It relates to feeling and to expressing our desires. It's the '**I want**' **i**mpulse**,** and about a basic level of sexuality; it's a sense of self, but at a basic level. We know that the First Chakra is about the basic instinct to survive. When we get to the sacral Chakra, we may still have the fears from the first chakra although probably a bit more subdued. At the Sacral Chakra we become more aware of our feelings and desires and needs.

This Sacral Chakra is about sensations. It's about pleasure, it's about sex, it's about I want and I will have; it expresses the Will to Feel, our feeling nature reaching out to others. It's about self-gratification. Relationships come very much to the fore in this chakra, but it is about gratification on different levels e.g. 'That's a nice dress', and we want that, so all the time it's about me, me, me at a very basic level. We know the water element is about emotions, sensations at a very basic level. When it's not balanced by higher wisdom or understanding, it manifests in things like the rampant sexuality we can see going on in the world now. People are still working from the sacral. We need to balance the chakras. When we move through the chakras, we begin to balance each one but if each chakra hasn't processed all the different levels, that is we haven't learned the soul lessons of each level to the highest degree, we can be totally out of balance.

This is why the world is in such a state of chaos, it is because it is out of balance, especially the sexual harassment that's going on. People are clearly finding it hard to control their feelings, their desires or their gratification. This is not about control in a negative way but by raising our awareness and by having consideration for others, we bring wisdom to bear and, at the same time, we bring ourselves back into balance.

When this Chakra is out of balance, it can affect the pancreas, the bladder, the spleen. We often hear of people, family or friends who are going through serious illnesses, think how courageous of them to choose a lifetime to process that condition. Whatever pain they go through, the discomfort and all the treatments, sometimes the relinquishing of life itself, that is the experience that they chose so they could learn to balance that chakra.

This chakra is also about reproduction. The generative organs are very important because to create and generate life is an awesome responsibility. In a sense the gift of this chakra is the gift of experiencing life through feelings and emotions. How we deal with this gift is up to us. Remember we are Spirit in embryo so although we reproduce life in embryo, we ourselves are Spirit in embryo. We're still learning, we are still babes in the spirit life, learning our way, feeling our way on this incredible journey we're all going through.

With the first chakra there is fear, with the second there is desire, the will to feel. But what happens when we don't get our desires, we don't get what we want? We become aggressive and angry. Anger is very much part of the second chakra. We start with fear and then we have anger, not a great start but on the other hand we need to know what fear and anger are and if we suppress anger that fire energy is going to go inward and then there's more fear and suppression and illness.

We are growing in Spirit and understanding. And this understanding enables us to look at the world and see it from the eyes of Spirit. Yes, it is chaotic, it is conflicting and there is so much ugliness around, but this is of our own doing (the wrong use of our Will) and not actually coming from our Spiritual self. This is because we are evolving through the Chakras.

This second chakra is very explorative because it makes us go more fully inside ourselves. It's exploring our inner world but also the outer world, because we can see how we are reacting to situations, to conditions, to people. What is happening in the world now? All the sexual harassment that is going on means we are working globally now with the second chakra. It's quite fascinating. We appear to have the polarities, that is the will, instinct, desire of the first two chakras, but in general without the love and wisdom of the higher chakras, thereby leaving us totally unbalanced.

When we talk about gratification and sexual abuse this is the second chakra which is the *Will to Feel*. We have mentioned the fear and the anger from the previous chakra – the First Chakra - which is the birth, the root of I AM at the basic level, this is the beginning of life; the Second Chakra is the feeling of life, the feeling of being. We have evolved enough to understand right and wrong. Therefore, if we went out and abused someone knowing it was wrong, we would attract restorative karma (karma that puts us back into balance). To get this deeper understanding is very important. If people knew or even acknowledged there was such a thing as karma, they might realize they were accountable, and refrain from acting in a negative way.

The First Chakra is also about self-protection, so we build whatever defenses we need for protection; the Second Chakra stock piles things because it is afraid (fear) to lose anything. Whenever there's a shortage of something, people go out and buy as much as they can of whatever item they consider vital. Stockpiling for protection is very much second chakra. I want, I cannot live without etc. In more modern-day times it's called hoarding. It expresses a lack of trust that our needs will be met.

If we are dealing with fear or anger, blockages can result here that could lead to illnesses. The Second Chakra can also create the 'drama queen' because it is about the sensations, self-gratification 'I desire, I want, I feel'. This is part of our sexuality and expressing our feelings and sensations. There are many ways to release sexual urges, it's not necessarily about going to bed with someone. It is about the expression of creativity, the expression of love. There are of course extremes, and this could also result in reckless behaviour. This is about getting a balanced creative energy.

The second chakra is very much involved in all relationships, not just male/female partnerships. If we allow our fear, anger, self-gratification to rule us, we could get into all kinds of difficulties in our relationships with friends, parents, family etc because those involved may be operating from different chakras and also different rays. This is why there is often such distress and conflict because everyone's coming from a different place. Sometimes it needs a flare-up to clear the air. Invariably, there are also times when relationships break down and there is a need to break away. Perhaps we can understand why in this day and age more and more couples are breaking up. It could well be that the karma between them is over or the relationship is no longer feeding the need for mutual growth.

A hundred years ago couples didn't separate, not perhaps because they didn't want to, but because they had no choice but to stay in relationships, happy or otherwise. Society dictated against women leaving their husbands or families. Sons and daughters didn't leave home until they were married whereas now they often leave as soon as they're 18 and can fend for themselves. This has naturally changed the nature of relationships and allowed for a greater freedom and respect between individuals. To reiterate, the second chakra is about expressing our needs, gratification, self-gratification, creativity and if we feel we're in an environment where we cannot express ourselves the desire is there to move on. A lot of what's going on today in society is very much related to the second chakra. So now let's go through the different levels:

## The root level of the Sacral chakra

This is about the awakenings of the feelings of desire. I want/ I don't want. The root of the sacral is a very basic primal feeling. Quite simply, 'I want that, and I want it now'. The stirring and awakening of feelings are at a basic and primal level because these feelings are not of the heart as the higher feelings are not awakened yet.

## The sacral level of the Sacral chakra

The feelings/desires related to this chakra are similar, for example, as to when we first fall in love; we can get a crush when we are young, and we can spend our time day dreaming about the other person. This can happen at any age. Girls have pop stars and boys pin ups and usually it's very OTT (over the top) but we don't necessarily do anything about it but just dream! As young children we can have crushes on people around us.

## The solar plexus level of the Sacral chakra

Maybe it's the first time when we can really engage with another and share those feelings. These feelings would be pretty normal, and the first stirrings and understanding of what relationships may lead to. So at this level it is really about exploring these new feelings and urges and also to be aware that these feelings can be a very potent force. At that sacral level if people start having sex when they are very young, they don't know how to control that, nor the emotions- talk about drama! The emotions are sky high; on the one hand it's lovely to be in love, but if this sexual energy is released and we don't know how to deal with that, things can get out of control.

## The heart level of the Sacral chakra

Then we come to the heart of the sacral where we begin to be much more aware of the people around us; we are aware of their feelings because they will make them known to us. This is not a one-sided thing. Relationships can be very demanding. However, if there is no real affection, understanding, or respect, it's difficult to know how to deal with that. This is where we start learning how to deal with other peoples' feelings at that level; respect and consideration has got to come into that, because we are developing the Heart Chakra at that basic level. Consideration is at a very basic level.

In relationships there will always be a difference of views. So, if somebody wants to go to the Mall, somebody wants to go the cinema, somebody wants to go for a nature walk, we make time for all of those. It's really about respecting and being considerate for others' feelings and it's not just about what I want. This is what the Heart Chakra is about and when we move into the Heart Chakra we begin to understand.

## The throat level of the Sacral chakra

The throat is about communication and expressing ourselves. This is also the opportunity for self-understanding as well as understanding others. It's about expressing our feelings at that basic level. Sometimes other people can be stronger-willed than us and appear to always have their own way. It's important here not to bottle up resentment or anger simply because we have not communicated our own feelings. Therefore the lesson in this chakra is to express our feelings and also showing consideration for others' feelings.

## The brow level of the Sacral chakra

The Brow is about perceptions (how we see life) and also understanding. How we perceive life gives us a responsibility about how we react to our feelings, sensations etc. We need to understand that going OTT like the drama queen and expressing reckless behavior isn't very sensible. So, it's about perceiving, understanding and seeing how our actions are affecting others. However, at this level we have the heart understanding so it's bringing all that into the picture.

## **The crown level of the Sacral chakra**

The Crown signifies enlightenment but remember we're at the basic level, so our enlightenment is going to bring us to a point where we cannot verbally spiritualize what we are going through because we don't yet have that higher understanding of the Crown and higher chakras. But it can bring us a kind of spiritual joy that we've got something right. For example, as we have been progressing through the other chakras, we may find ourselves with a crowd of people or family and friends and there's a 'Ah that feels good' kind of feeling, its harmonious, it's joyful. We may not understand what we are feeling except that we are in a harmonious situation. It's a similar feeling when we inexplicably become aware of joy or happiness in our group soul. We are all sharing that harmony and joy.

## **Conclusion**

The gift of the second chakra, the Sacral, is expressiveness, creativity and flair. This is about our feelings and sensations; the lesson is to understand our reactions to our inner and outer worlds and decide how we are going to express these reactions. Feelings originating here are generally softer than feelings stemming from the first chakra, and the healthy way to work them out is through creative or emotive expression. It is also about understanding our passions and how to express them.

# The Third Chakra is the Solar Plexus

This is the Will to Think – Will, Purpose,
Strength, The Power of Imagination

> **Influences & Links:**
>
> Colour is Yellow (see Chapter 6 for more explanation on the colour)
>
> Planet is Jupiter
> Jupiter is the planet of expansion allowing us to use our creativity to expand our consciousness and at the same time to balance our emotions.
>
> Element is Fire
> The Element is Fire because it brings us the opportunity to understand Love. In other words, to understand the difference between sentimentality, mawkishness and the true feelings of the heart. The Fire element also gives us the energy, the force, the power to create and balance. It is the Will to Think creatively and to understand.
>
> Soul Lesson
> The soul lesson for this chakra is the opportunity to balance our emotions. The Fire element in this chakra means that our emotions can be like a see-saw, up one minute, down the next. Love, at this level, is more often than not sentimentality and emotionalism, with our desires driving us on. It is about understanding our power and passions. This is also a lesson for using our thoughts in a creative way.
>
> Possible physical problems:
> Problems with pancreas, including diabetes and hypoglycaemia, ulcers, digestive problems, liver, hepatitis, liver cancer, hiatus hernia, gallstones, haemorrhoids, varicose veins, spleen.

## **The Third Chakra – The Solar Plexus - Pancreas**

The solar plexus deals with all our emotions. We need to balance the emotions; we're coming up from the fear of the first chakra, the root, the primordial will to survive, then with the second chakra, the sacral, the will to feel, the desire which can be creative, but it can also be destructive. This chakra can also stir up our anger and guilt levels. The mind is involved but at a much more basic and lower level. The second and third chakra are the very active chakras in humanity today. Those going through this chakra often feel worried and concerned about the future and can be demanding emotionally and mentally, they feel they are missing out on something. This chakra is about the **Will to Think**.

The solar plexus is connected to the 3$^{rd}$ Ray of Active Intelligence and Adaptability. This is the will to think at a more basic level and can often give way to out of control emotions, desires, fear and anger. The associated planet is Jupiter, the planet of expansion. Jupiter is the Great Benefactor which enables us to explore and expand our creativity. Unless we've got a well-developed and balanced first and second chakra we could get into difficulties when we come up to the third chakra because that fear, that anger, that desire, the will to be and the will to live is going to be exaggerated in the Solar Plexus.

From the fear comes the anger and often guilt. If we're afraid of something and we don't know how to control those emotions, then we have a problem. The Solar Plexus, when it's beautifully balanced, is most creative and proactive; the problem with the Solar Plexus is we are often reactive; there is the other opposite of course and that is being inactive. When we give way to that fear or anger it is almost like a paralyzing feeling, we can be afraid to do anything - how many people go through life seemingly doing nothing? But also, because the Solar Plexus is all about the emotions there are times when we run out of energy and we haven't got the stamina to keep going. Many souls fail at this point because although they have the impulse to create and survive, they haven't got the stamina that goes with it.

When we're faced with those fears we tend to go back to that root and that survival impulse. Therefore, we react from that fear and anger because we haven't developed yet the wisdom that we need to bring about the balance needed to react appropriately to situations. Consequently, we are incapable of being proactive and tactful. We can tell that globally the consciousness of humanity is trying to find that creativity but through chaos and conflict. The will to survive, the will to desire, the will to think creatively through the third chakra **is there** and we can see it in different factions of humanity but what's holding it back is fear and anger from the first and second chakra. The power of imagination is also part of the third chakra with the purpose and the strength. It's connected to the element of fire which is the life force energy.

If we have a balanced 1st and 2nd Chakra, in the 3rd Chakra we have a wonderful opportunity to create. We have survived, we have balanced our desires and urges. The 2nd chakra is concerned with procreation, which is about creating and using our imagination to make something beautiful out of life, out of ourselves as long as it's balanced. Remember, we may have moved up the chakras but that does not necessarily mean that we have balanced all the different levels in each chakra. Therefore, those feelings of survival and desire may still be lurking. Then there can also be those feelings of guilt, or shame, or feelings of being uncomfortable from something that we may have done or said in the past.

At this level it is possible that the personality isn't as yet conscious of the Soul or the Spirit. Therefore, it is more in control over our actions and our feelings. In the 3rd chakra we begin to be a bit more aware of consciousness but at that point we're not sure what that consciousness is or what it means. We don't have that fundamental understanding. Around the world today we can see evidence of an imbalance in the 3rd Chakra. So many are ruled by their emotions and desires.

Until we become more aware of the Soul consciousness in this chakra we are still ruled by our personality or ego. (The personality rules the three lower chakras). This Chakra is about the will to think, the purpose, the strength and the power of imagination. Remember that the influence of the 3rd Ray is quite powerful and has the fire behind it. This is where we find bullies and dictators. These personalities can think 'It's **MY** purpose, **MY** strength, **I** know I'm right, I don't care if you, you and you don't like it, I know I'm right'. We can see why individuals emerge as dictators and this is because they have not yet fully developed the heart, the wisdom, the love and understanding but instead they are ruled by their ego, their emotions and desires.

Remember there's love too in the 3rd Chakra but on a different level. There's the love of the personality, the love of beautiful things, the love and desire coming up from the 2nd Chakra and it's the beginnings of those gentler feelings and the development of the 3rd chakra. We learn how to be proactive in that beauty. But it's when it's not balanced and still underdeveloped then we get into trouble.

This is a tremendous chakra to go through. It is affecting so many millions of souls around the world. Of course, there are others who have moved on and are developing the higher chakras. We usually appreciate the wisdom and understanding of these souls.

The 3rd Chakra is about being proactive but unfortunately if it's not well balanced it'll be reactive in anger, in jealousy, envy and hurt. People react when they're hurt, and they can be very bitter and defensive. Sometimes it's hard enough to understand ourselves, let alone trying to understand what humanity is going through. It's much easier of course if we can be detached from the world and merely observe, with that sense of detachment, what is happening around us, whether it's the environment, nature, politics or the business and economic worlds.

This is a wonderful chakra but my goodness it is a tough one. On the Soul journey the 1st chakra, roughly speaking, could be compared to 1-7 years of age; it's our beginning, our root. From the ages of 7-14 we are getting to know about feelings, relationships, but between the ages of 14-21 we could say we begin to understand ourselves a little better, we begin to see all the different options that are available to us.

As we grow in understanding we realise that often there is a need to choose and make decisions. What are we going to do in life? Where do we want to go with our relationships? This just parallels where humanity is. **Humanity has come to a point where it needs to choose, make decisions and take responsibility.**

Do we choose to follow bullies or dictators? We have been indoctrinated for so long we have forgotten that our reality is only the perceptions we have acquired through our indoctrination. However, as we develop the power to think and the power of imagination, now is the time to make those choices in a more detached and balanced way.

In the 3rd chakra we also have the opportunity to work towards self-acceptance, self-worth and confidence. On the other side of the coin we may experience low self-esteem and lack of confidence and that is because fear and anger may well up within us, putting the 3rd chakra out of kilter. The problem here is that we end up with people not valuing themselves. Just think when the 3rd chakra is balanced with all the others how wonderful that will be. We need to accept ourselves. Talk about power! That's what we're aiming at by unfolding and balancing this chakra. Self-empowerment!

There is also a downside to this. There are times when some people just do not have the energy to fight, to stand up for themselves in a conflicting situation, especially if this keeps going on every day relentlessly. The energy to fight is not there so we just roll over. Life is a misery, it adds to our feelings of low self-worth, low self-esteem and frustration. This leads to self-doubt. But we also need to remember the other aspect of this, which is equally as dangerous to our growth, and that is the inflated ego. In this chakra we are still dealing with the personality and this isn't just about bullies or being dictatorial this is about an inflated ego. Our ego tells us 'We think we're right; we know we're right' and that means everybody else is wrong. The inflated ego is a product of a 3rd Chakra imbalance.

In the 3rd chakra we have the power to choose; we may not have developed all the different levels of the two previous chakras, but we may have gained some sort of balance within the chakras. If we are aware of our life's purpose (and very few people are) we can choose to continue this or we can choose to just live out our karma if we haven't got the energy or the imagination to completely live our life's purpose. We just live to work through our karma although most of the time this is unconsciously.

The 3rd chakra can produce health problems with the pancreas, ulcers, liver, kidneys, gallstones, diabetes, anything that affects the stomach and abdomen. It doesn't mean that everybody gets them. What needs to be remembered is that conditions come so that we can do something about them, that we can learn from the experience.

## The root level of the Solar Plexus chakra

The solar plexus is about emotions and creativity. At the root level of this chakra we start to rationalise our fears, our sensations from the Root and Sacral chakras. It could be said that at this level we are learning more about who we are. We know that the root is about the primal survival instinct and the sacral is about sensations and dealing with those desires. It needs to be remembered that at this point we are still only dealing with the personality.

## The sacral level of the Solar Plexus chakra

The sacral is all about relationships in general, not only sexual. In that context, with the solar plexus chakra being active and proactive, we are now more confident, shall we say, in developing relationships. This is about getting to know others in different relationships. It is also about understanding our own reactions and dealing with situations that require choices to be made. The sacral level in the solar plexus is all about our desires, our instincts and our reactions.

## The solar plexus level of the Solar Plexus chakra

This is all about personality emotions. If we haven't yet developed a loving heart, it's going to be quite a selfish love. This is about me, me wanting to do something and taking control over others' feelings or wishes. At this level it may not occur to us to ask someone what they would like to do because we may not yet have developed the power of thinking or imagination about adaptability. The intelligence, the mind may be active but the adaptability, the consideration isn't there yet.

## The heart level of the Solar Plexus chakra

When we start developing at this level, different emotions come in. The heart is love but here it's still emotional love. It's sentimentality, it's gushy, it's mawkishness. The feeling is there as we have already connected with a heart feeling, but it tends to be very emotional and sentimental and there could be a tendency to be selfish. Our love can still be about 'me'. Do we put an emotional hold on others?

In the Sacral Chakra, we talked about the drama queen where this is exaggerated. The drama queen will create a scenario which will leave people feeling overwhelmed because their emotions are gushing all over the place. When we get the first stirrings of love, if we are not stable, we will not be sure how to handle that love.

Developing the heart level of the solar plexus is a tough one because emotions are involved. If we look at the world, it is clear so many people don't know how to deal with emotions because people can't always talk about emotions. Because the emotions aren't balanced, they can get into sentimentality and gushiness, manipulations, and drama queens getting their own way. It's not difficult to see how the world is in such a state of flux.

## The throat level of the Solar Plexus chakra

The throat is about communication and expressing ourselves. At this level it is also about justification. Justifying what we say and how we act and express this. We express our emotions from another level of understanding.

This is not just about understanding ourselves better but also because we need to justify ourselves to others. So, the throat level is expressing our justifiability because that's important to us. It is a justification to ourselves, it's not just to other people. It's self-justification; we could be feeling uncomfortable about something we may have said or done, and we go away thinking, 'I feel a bit uncomfortable about that, should I have said that or done that.' If that is the case, we may feel a need for justification.

In a beautiful way, it is also about expressing our emotions, our passions. It is about feeling that self-empowerment and expressing it.

## **The brow level of the Solar Plexus chakra**

The Brow is about perceiving how we interact with life and with people. Our perception and because it is based on our indoctrination can also be a delusion. It's balancing what is delusion and what is real. This is not easy to fathom because our conditioning and our emotions are based on our indoctrination of life from the moment we are born. If our emotions and our chakras are not balanced and we do not question or even understand our conditioning or indoctrination, the chances are that we will not be able to have clarity in how we perceive life. We need to ask ourselves is our perception real or delusional? Therefore the Brow centre is about bringing clarity to discern the delusional to the real, so that our perception in life is real and true. This is huge because remember we are only at the solar plexus which is still the level of personality and at that level, ego comes into it. We have to justify ourselves but part of us is also saying 'But is that delusional or is it real? We remember that the solar plexus is the power of imagination, not intuition and still the basic I AM. All we understand at this level is that we are surviving. This is a very important level to get to.

## **The crown level in the Solar Plexus chakra**

Then we get to the Crown Chakra which relates to enlightenment or consciousness. Having come through all the levels of this chakra, we get to the crown where it takes all the information and knowledge of the first three chakras. We're balancing all that loving and caring, then we move to expressing ourselves and finally we get to the justification of that. What the crown does at that level is like a systemization of spirituality. What I mean by systemisation is that we sort out what we have learned, what we have experienced through the soul lessons of the different levels in this chakra and puts it in a more structured manner. Remember this Chakra is influenced by the 3$^{rd}$ Ray of Active Intelligence & Adaptability. This means that the influence of the 3$^{rd}$ Ray makes it all whole or harmonized and this is where all the pieces fit together thus far.

So this is what the Crown level in the Solar Plexus does. It goes through all the different levels and makes sense of it all, systemizing everything that we've gone through at that level.

## **Conclusion:**

This chakra is directly connected with the astral/emotional body and serve as the conduit and escape valve for the emotional energies generated in the astral body. Emotions flow through this instrument. It is said in theosophical writings, that this chakra became fully functional during the fourth root-race on Atlantis. It is the gathering point for all of the lower energies below the diaphragm before they are necessarily transmuted and transferred to the Heart Chakra by the aspirant-disciple on the Path.

# The Fourth Chakra is the Heart

**It is the Will to Love – Unconditional Love**

> **Influences & Links:**
>
> <u>Colour is Green</u> (see Chapter 6 for more explanation on the colour)
>
> <u>Planets are Sun/Venus</u>
> The Sun is our life-force. Venus is the planet of beauty and joy, of human love and happiness.
>
> <u>Element is Air</u>
> This element helps to bring about the understanding mind in the Heart Chakra. Discerning between the outer mind which needs to control us, and the higher mind which brings us the wisdom of the soul, and also the love and compassion which we have unfolded by the time we rise up to the 4th Chakra – the Heart. The Air Element enable us to clear our minds from dross and understand the difference between real Love and sentimental love.
>
> <u>Soul Lesson</u>
> This lesson is about understanding real love and compassion. This is about unconditional Love. Not the gushy, emotionalism and sentimentality of the 3rd Chakra, the Solar Plexus. The lesson is also how to deal with life's problems in a caring, considerate and loving way. It is also about balancing our personality and preparing ourselves for a higher consciousness.
>
> <u>Possible physical problems:</u>
> Coronary artery disease. Thymus, Immune system.

## **The Fourth Chakra – The Heart - Thymus**

The 4th chakra is the Heart and the balance of everything. It is located in the centre of the chest. The colour associated with the heart is Green which is the colour of harmony and balance and it's connected to the 4th Ray of Harmony through Conflict. Look at nature, there's nothing more harmonious than nature and just look at how all the different shades of green blend together. It is through conflict and chaos that we eventually find that harmony, that peace within. With all the chaos and conflict going on around us now it is not surprising to learn that it is the 4$^{th}$ Ray of Harmony through Conflict that is influencing humanity.

The heart chakra is the chakra that is striving for balance, for harmony, and in a sense perfection at a higher level. Perfection is the ideal we are aiming for and this will come when we've completed and evolved through all our chakras, initiations etc. When we accomplish the soul lessons of this chakra the opportunity to attain this balance is there at a deeper level. The three lower chakras are related to the personality so therefore the heart, the fourth chakra, is balancing together the result of the understanding and lessons of the three lower chakras. The element of this Chakra is Air and the planets are the Sun and Venus. The Sun brings us positivity, it brings us life. Venus is the planet of beauty and joy. This means that the heart, in a sense, is bringing love and understanding to the lower diaphragm. The thymus gland is ruled by the Heart Chakra.

To recap - first there is the Will to Survive of the Root Chakra and this was about, instinct, survival, me, me, me, and fear. The Sacral Chakra is the desire, our sensations, the sexual urges which can be creative on the positive side and procreation. We look at humanity now, and we see how people are still surviving. We have been surviving millions of years. That is the Will to Be, the I AM at a very basic level. What we need to remember always with all the chakras is that the soul consciousness is not there at the root, but what is there from the very, very beginning of humanity is the essence of Spirit. However Spirit does not know itself. It is experimenting with life. It is Spirit unmanifested. It has not yet unfolded to its true potential. It is only by going through the fears, the desires, the sensations and the emotions that we get to the heart which is about understanding and unconditional love. This is what we're aiming for - to reach that level of unconditional love, where the love is not just for self, it is for others, and all life as well.

At this level we begin to understand group consciousness and group co-operation. This group could be anything; it could be a family group, a community group, a tribal group, whatever. It's about understanding that it's not just about me. It's not about **my** urges or desires, or **my** sensations, it's about the realisation and understanding that we are part of a group, whatever group that may be. It is about showing consideration and compassion for others. We may have strong desires or strong feelings about something but when the Heart Chakra starts developing we begin to realize we need to have a bit more consideration, more understanding and more empathy with other people. The unfolding of our Heart Chakra moves us towards unconditional love for others, but at this level it's still very much a sense of self love. We **do** have sympathy for others, but we can only judge that from how it affects us and our perception.

What the heart centre at this level brings is an empathy or the beginnings of it for others, outside ourselves. We can hear a sad story and we feel sympathy, but we can only relate to this from our own level of understanding coming through the emotions, sensations, desires and fears.

There are differences in the feelings of loving because we are learning the lesson of real love, not sentimentality, not the emotionalism of the 3rd Chakra, but rather unconditional self-less love. We see many groups around the world who are selflessly giving of their service and their skills to help those in need. This is about group co-operation, group consciousness. Where the heart has been touched this is where group co-operation and group service come in.

The wonderful thing about evolving through the Chakras is that we can keep moving on even though we may not have completed all the seven levels of each Chakra. The wisdom, the understanding and compassionate lessons of the Heart Chakra will give us the courage, strength and wisdom to go back and finish off any levels of preceding Chakras that have not yet been completed.

There are different levels of development in humanity. We truly cannot judge another at soul level! We have no idea as to what levels of development and evolution that soul, that individual is going through. Individuals could be undergoing soul lessons on different levels of the chakras and also initiations. Sometimes we need to reach the Heart Chakra to attain that understanding, that compassion, that courage to go back and re-take those lessons.

We always need to remember that what we see when we look at others, when we look at circumstances around us, is our perception, we're seeing that will to survive, the desire, me, me, me – self-preservation. That's what we see; that's why so often the teachers of wisdom tell us 'do not judge' – we dare not judge - because we really do not understand. We know that the teachers look at a soul, an individual and observe the chakras because the chakras are like spinning wheels, up and up and up through the body the spinal cord and if that person is balancing and working and developing the chakras, the spinning is more intense and brighter; it also vibrates to a sound because we all have a sound; all of us also have a note and a colour. So, the lesser we are evolved a paler and less rich shade of colour can occur and be seen by clairvoyants. We get to a point where Light itself is pale but it's luminous and such a force of power. However, we do get colours that appear dull and lifeless, and that is because some chakras are not yet fully developed.

Our need, as we develop and unfold the Heart Chakra, is to find harmony and unity because it is necessary to unify all the chakras; it's not just about one or some being in balance. We need to unite *all* the Chakras This is what the lessons of all the chakras mean; we have to unite them and bring them up that spinal cord, from Root to Crown, so that we emerge as a Luminous Spiritual Being.

When we get to the Heart Chakra we also develop compassion, which is an aspect of love and when we love with compassion this is selfless and affects all life. Coming to this chakra we have a little bit more understanding of the previous three chakras and therefore we begin to work more cohesively with the soul. The soul is in more cohesion with itself in this Chakra, although it hasn't yet developed the knowledge of the Crown in its fullest sense. However, it does understand the cohesion of all the different chakras, the will to be, the will to survive, the will to do, the I AM, the desires, the urges and it begins to try and put all this into some form of cohesion.

*Cohesion* is a very important word in describing where we're at when we start unfolding the Heart Chakra. With cohesion there is also projection.

When we reach this understanding of the heart and we start using the knowledge that we have acquired at soul level to this point, we begin to act. Remember everything that we are, all that we are right now, everything we say, everything we think, everything we feel, everything now is the total sum of everything we have ever learnt. Yes, we have perceptions that have been obtained from belief systems and from indoctrination. We have perceptions imported from our family unit, community, race, culture, nations. The I AM is not just the I AM in this lifetime, it's the cumulative I AM from all the lessons learned and qualities unfolded along the Path. But, how do we deal with those lessons? Do we put them into action, or do we put them in a box? There comes a point in our evolution when we realise we need to free ourselves from all those little boxes. This is what I mean about cohesion and unity, this is what happens when we reach and unfold the Heart Chakra.

We also project who we are and what we are, and we attract by our projections. Our Soul knows what lessons we need and will bring people into our lives to help us learn those lessons. We can be totally on our own under many circumstances, but we can never be lonely when we have found the Spirit within. We have people in our lives because we need to learn from those relationships, so we attract into our lives people we need to learn from. When we no longer need them, they fade away. Life has a way of disentangling us from situations or people when those lessons are learned. And because we come from the heart this usually happens in a more harmonious and loving way. This is also about projection and magnetism. Finding the spirit within doesn't mean we need to be hermits, the days of convents and monasteries are behind us, we have to live in the world, but we can choose. We may face many challenging situations, but we can choose how we react. The unfolding of the Heart Chakra gives us this understanding.

The Heart Chakra also gives us the Will to Serve. Our work is to be of service to others and we can do that in whatever shape or form life takes us, because it isn't work anymore it is life. Service becomes our life; our life becomes our service. It's all the same. That's what the heart does. When we start working on the heart and opening up at that level, there's that cohesion, the yin and the yang. The 3$^{rd}$ Chakra gave us the emotions, so we are very much aware of all the different emotions, positive and negative. But it's the 4$^{th}$ Chakra that teaches us about real love. We surrender to love. The heart brings us the tolerance towards other people, patience with other people and sometimes disagreements with other people, but we have to have that respect to say 'actually I don't agree with any of that but I respect your right to have your opinion.'

Respect for each other's beliefs. We need to be open – openness is another aspect of the heart chakra, to be open to another's love, to another's teaching or knowledge or to another's **Being**. They have a right to be on earth just as we have. If we could do that what a wonderful world it would be, and that's all part of what is unfolding in the heart chakra.

Sometimes if we are too open and sensitive we could be empathetic and sympathetic to every problem that anybody might have and at times this can leave us at the mercy of other people's emotions. In other words, we could be ultra-sensitive which leaves us wide open to others' manipulation. This happens when the Heart Chakra is too open, and we haven't balanced it with wisdom. We may well ask what is wrong with an open heart. Nothing, but if we don't balance it with wisdom we are at the mercy of others' emotions and whims. In so doing we can also deplete our own energy as we are giving and giving. This does not necessarily serve us nor others. By giving in to others' emotions we may not be helping them. In a sense, doing this is going down into the 3$^{rd}$ chakra again which means we haven't balanced that. All the chakras have their imbalances and it's about finding that unity and cohesion in them.

## The root level of the Heart chakra

The Root Chakra is about instinct, survival, fear. We all want to survive even at the heart level. Remember the heart is about group co-operation. It is also about socializing, it's about being a part of a group, making ourself agreeable, wanting to belong to any group whatever that may be. There may be times when we suppress our own thoughts and feelings because we want to be in that group, and we don't want them to dislike us. Socializing is part of the root level of the Heart Chakra. What we are doing is establishing our place in society or group. This is necessary as it is our Will to Survive. It could be the family, work, school or community, wherever we feel that need to establish our place because that's our survival instinct within the heart. The heart is about being part of a group situation and the heart wants to give love and be loved but remember we're still at the root (survival) of the heart and we haven't yet necessarily developed inner wisdom.

## **The sacral level of the Heart chakra**

The sacral is about the urges and desires that we have. It is also about creativity. This is about friendships because at the level of sensations and feelings of the sacral, we begin to form relationships in whatever situation we may find ourselves. The sacral in the heart is about friendships and relationships in different forms and our place within them, whether it's friends, siblings, neighbours, groups or networking with other people. With some people we gel, with others we don't, and this lesson is about understanding that. Because the heart is involved it's how we react to all this and if we haven't quite balanced the emotions in the 3rd Chakra, this will have an impact on how we develop those friendships. We need to transmute possible feelings of jealousy and envy. If we don't, then we may step into the role of the victim who asks, 'Is the whole world against me? When anything goes wrong in people's lives, for example, the washing machine breaks down or the car doesn't start in the morning, 'The world is against me.' The universe isn't against us, these things just happen to everybody but if we are OTT and we haven't balanced our emotions we **do** feel the whole world is against us. So, the sacral in the heart is about understanding relationships in their different forms.

## **The solar plexus level of the Heart chakra**

The solar plexus is about our emotions. This is about the desire to please people and how people react to us. When our emotions are involved these two factors can be very dangerous unless we can act in a positive way. The danger here is that we could be out of balance. We know of people who get tearful at the slightest little thing, or they may take umbrage and become angry and hurt and they react from these emotions. At this level and because the 5$^{th}$ Chakra, the Throat, has not yet been developed things are said that can be very devastating for other people. Sometimes people could end up in tears or in anger because our desires or sensations are involved.

How often do we see people saying or doing things out of anger arising from fear? Again, it is about getting that balance and it's also because it's sensationalism. We want people to think well of us and to understand us. People often say, 'They just don't understand me?' We have a real desire here to be understood. We want to be accepted. We want to be acknowledged for who we are. We want to be loved. We want to belong. This is what the Solar Plexus level in the Heart Chakra is about.

It is a wonderful chakra in many ways because all our feelings and emotions are there but, until we balance the see-saw, we could be in a lot of difficulty. We want to get to the point where our love is unconditional. However, here at the solar plexus level, it's still very much conditional love. We will, as we rise up the Chakras, find that aspect within ourselves where we will accept ourselves in totality and not feel threatened or challenged by another's skills, capabilities or ideas. This is total acceptance of who we are at peace with ourselves, wherever we are.

## **The heart level of the Heart chakra**

The heart of the heart is a beautiful place to be because it's that harmony, that balance in life and as we get to the heart there's more stability. The see-saw is not so extreme with our emotions or our anger or fear, it's more stable. This is because there's more wisdom and understanding. Our wisdom is beginning to unfold. However, there could be a risk here. The risk is that as we start balancing life, we could become self-righteous or arrogant. Sometimes people take great pride in saying 'I don't change, I'm the same person I was years ago'. However, we know that in life, it is in the meeting of challenges that we learn and go forward. Change is a motivating factor in growing spiritually.

There are times when a lack of motivation could lead to boredom. Perhaps we are just too content or selfish to interest ourselves in other people's lives. There are many different reasons behind the risk of boredom. There's always a risk that we could be too stable, too harmonious and that could produce the risk of complacency. We need lessons and challenges in life. However, we do know that at that deeper level, the Soul is actively working for our evolution and we can only remain in a seemingly dormant spot for a period of time and then life will throw its challenges at us.

## The throat level of the Heart chakra

The Throat Chakra is about communication, expression. At this level we have now got to start expressing the cohesion, the unity, balance and stability that has been learned through all the different chakras. It's wonderful if we are able to do that and express ourselves; to be able to speak our truth from that lovely space of harmony and balance. But if we have not balanced the previous levels, remember people can be at the Throat Chakra without having balanced some of the levels of the other chakras – so what's going to happen then? There could be insincerity in what we are say, or we could be bombastic, pushy and intolerant because we feel that what we are saying or thinking is right- and we may be right but that's not the point, it could be uninformed. It could also be very selfish and hurtful because if we haven't balanced our emotions, our desires, our instinct for survival then our expressions could be very impactful.

We may be a compassionate person but, in our compassion, we could say the wrong thing. We could say to somebody, 'look I'm really sorry about what you're going through, I really appreciate it, but you've only got yourself to blame. You shouldn't have done that, why are you in this mess. Look at yourself.' This is very judgmental and harsh because we haven't yet balanced the wisdom aspect of ourselves. This is where we have to be aware of responsibility. Responsibility is such an important law; it's one of the Laws of Karma – the Law of Responsibility. It's responsibility not just in what we do but also what we say. We can sometimes hurt people more by what we say than what we actually do. Words can be like poisoned darts. Afterwards we can go away thinking 'Well I told her, I had to be upfront with her'. People pride themselves on being upfront. 'You get the truth from me; you won't get anything else.' But we can devastate someone by being upfront and true.

We have to be so careful about how we say things. When we say things in a kind, compassionate way, all parties involved move forward in a harmonious way – back to the heart for harmony all the time and for balance because it's the middle chakra. We need to be more and more aware of how we express ourselves. People don't mean to be hurtful or devastate someone but if we get the 'wilting lilies' who are so caught up in their emotions any strong word will set them off or completely devastate them because their solar plexus is so open it goes straight in.

It reinforces the old belief about pausing before you react, this is so very important. It only takes a second. We can train ourselves to pause and then we are in a better, more balanced position when it comes to what we say and how we say it, which is what matters. People get themselves into trouble and hurt others by over reacting and not thinking. It's just not thinking before they speak. Tact, consideration in our speech is so important.

## **The brow level of the Heart chakra**

The Brow Chakra is about perception, how we see things, how we perceive and, in some ways, how we judge things. The third eye (the brow level) is where we do our thinking and perceiving people and events. Once again, if we have not balanced our emotions, transmuted our fears or balanced our desires this can be a very judgmental chakra until we learn how to balance it. We see things in a very judgemental way because we all have different perceptions and these usually come from our indoctrination and conditioning in life from the very moment we are born. How do we see and judge life? We can all look at a picture and see different things in it. The Brow level is important in the Heart Chakra because, when we find that harmony and cohesion and unity as we evolve, we bring that into our perception thereby changing the way we see and perceive others and life itself. The Heart Chakra gives us the opportunity to learn how to have a clearer understanding of what we are perceiving, what is in front of us. We then get a clearer picture of what is going on around us, because the heart which is by now more stable and balanced is giving us that clarity. What we're getting here and now is clarity, not as much as we will get when we get to the Brow of the Brow but the fact that we are opening our heart will give us a clearer understanding. This work cannot be hurried because if we want to do it properly we have got to do it slowly.

## **The crown level of the Heart chakra**

When we get to the Crown level of the Heart Chakra what we're really looking for is spiritual harmony because this level is about knowing, and the heart is about understanding and wisdom. When we get to this level of the heart we are beginning to understand we are Spirit. We may not know we are Spirit, or rather we may not have realized it yet, but we are beginning to understand more about spirituality. It's about that spiritual harmony that we're all seeking. The knowing of the knowing doesn't come until we reach the Crown of the Crown, the Absolute higher consciousness.

But here, at this level, it is wisdom, it's spiritual wisdom, spiritual harmony and finding our connection all the way down, looking back and asking – who am I? How did I get here, where did I come from, what have I learnt, what lessons have I done really well, what other lessons have I still to work on? it's been a long, long, long journey and many people are still at the sacral and solar plexus; some could say they're reaching the heart and one or two levels possibly of the throat but when we get to the Crown it has been a very long journey. Unfolding and evolving through all the chakras could take hundreds of life-times. The first three chakras involve the personality and they are very unevolved at that stage. When we reach the Crown level of the Heart Chakra that lovely spiritual knowledge, spiritual understanding is beginning to take shape. But it's not complete. Let's not think the Crown of the heart is the be all and end all, it's not. It's the harmony, the balance, the cohesion of what we have learned thus far.

## **Conclusion:**

This is the chakra that balances the lower and upper triangles. The three chakras of the Personality (Root, Sacral, Solar Plexus) and the three chakras of the Spirit (Throat, Brow, Crown). This is the chakra that steadies us. It has been a long trek, a long battle to get here, but at this level the Warrior can look back and say, 'I have triumphed and overcome, now I am ready to move on'.

# The Fifth Chakra
is the Throat

**This is about Communication - The Will to Express - I Speak**

> **Influences & Links:**
>
> <u>Colour is Blue</u> (see Chapter 6 for more explanation on the colour)
>
> <u>Planet is Mercury</u>
> Mercury is known as the Messenger of the Gods. The planet of divine wisdom and intelligence, rules all form of communication.
>
> <u>Element is the Ether</u>
> The spiritual substance or space in which we breathe, move and have our being.
>
> <u>Soul Lesson</u>
> After the soul lesson of the Heart Chakra – 4th- where the heart has awakened to unconditional love, the throat chakra brings us the lesson of unity. Unity embraces love for other kingdoms of nature. This recognises the brotherhood of all life. It teaches us to express love in a positive and loving manner, speaking our truth, sounding our note.
>
> <u>Possible physical problems</u>
> Tonsillitis - thyroid, throat cancer, disorders of the jaw, neck & sinus

## The Fifth Chakra – The Throat - Thyroid

The Throat Chakra is the Chakra of communication, our Will to Express ourselves in different ways. It is connected to the 5th Ray of Concrete Knowledge and Science and this Ray has great influence because it is the realization of this Concrete Knowledge that enables us to speak our truth. So, here we have the power, the will to express that realization.

The throat chakra is also very creative, it's aligned to the sacral. All the chakras have a link to other chakras. When we have balanced the Solar Plexus and developed the understanding and wisdom of the Heart, think how creative we can be once we express our creativity. This is the beauty of this chakra. When we express our creativity, to be able to express who we are, this is an incredible empowerment, self-empowerment because we know who we are, and we are expressing our creativity. If we've balanced the 1st and 2nd Chakras which are the root of our fears, our sensations, we've got the beautiful balance of the creativity, of the emotions and feelings of the solar plexus working together in harmony. We are bringing all that into the heart, which is open in compassion, in love, in understanding; we're able to express all that beautifully. That's what we're all aiming for and we will get there, it just takes time and spiritual patience. This is what the 5th chakra is about, its ultimate aim, its work and its function.

In the ancient wisdom the throat centre was, and is, considered sacred and holy. One of the lessons of the early mystery schools was to guard the tongue and also to use speech accurately and with power because it is holy. It is connected to the solar plexus and links with our creativity. This is sounding our own spiritual note. Every individual learns in the course of experience to sound his or her soul note or word. In other words, this is about speaking our truth. These are all the positive aspects of the throat chakra. This is our function; this is our aim and goal. But to get there we have to go through the journey of the path of the soul through the chakras, and we cannot deny all the negativity that exists because we live in a human world. Think of the opposite of not being able to speak your truth. How frustrating and limiting! We couldn't grow or move at all. Think also about guarding the tongue because if we don't guard our tongue, we can devastate people by the things we say and how we say them, often without realizing it. Sometimes we do realize; we want to speak with mischief. There are times also when speaking our truth is fine for us but it's *how* we speak it that's important. So often people say, 'I'm going to tell you exactly how it is.' This is fine. To be honest, to be truthful is a wonderful quality **but it is how we say it that matters.**

It is also helpful to ask ourselves - what is our truth? Is it coming from our own perceptions, based on past indoctrination and conditioning? Speaking our truth isn't always necessarily coming from our spiritual Higher Self. If we haven't developed the Heart Chakra properly there may be times where we can have the compassion, the understanding and the tolerance for other people, but the personality can hijack the Throat Chakra to manipulate. This is because this Chakra can be very forceful. If we're dominated by a need to take over, we can be very forceful in what we say, and we can literally flatten people. There may be those who have not been able to express what they feel or think and will just keep quiet for the sake of not causing trouble. So again, it's *how* we speak our truth and always being wary about the origin of what we feel coming into our hearts and minds. Even on the spiritual path we invariably fail on this. We can get caught up in what's known as 'spiritual dogma' quoting various teachers or writers believing that only what they say is Truth. Now that could become a dogma and it may mean that we close our minds to other perspectives. Expressing ourselves is not as easy as just saying 'I'm going to speak my truth.' It requires a lot of wisdom, sensitivity, patience and pausing.

The beauty of the spiritual life is having the wisdom and the understanding not to get into any kind of dogma. We may think that the orthodox churches are full of dogma, but so is the spiritual path. The 'straight and narrow path' can be more dangerous because we think we have a window, a door or a gateway to some spiritual aspect of truth, only to find that we have fallen into the pit of dogma without knowing it and have come to that point in all sincerity. But what is the point when sincerity becomes dogma? We need to be ever watchful as we continue the journey. It's the journey of the soul while we're still in the earthly round of incarnations. It's just a journey – what we learn from all our experiences is just part of that journey. We can read many books, listen to many teachers, philosophising to our heart's content, all this is great. This is fine for a while and then we get to a point where we think 'thank you for those experiences, thank you for what you have taught me, I've learned a great deal, but I now need to move on.'

This is the T-junction to which the Throat Chakra brings us. There are different ways to go and we have to stop. Evolving through the previous four Chakras we have attained a balance, an understanding. It is important to remember at this stage that as yet we have not completely activated all the chakras fully. We need to keep coming back, lifetime after lifetime, cleansing, clearing, learning. We need the wisdom of the heart and the courage to deal with the fears arising from the mis-use of energies in the Root Chakra, we need to come back to deal with feelings, sensations, the negative emotions, the anger, the hatred and the bitterness.

The understanding of the Heart Chakra helps us to go through all the experiences necessary, but it is when we get to the throat that we truly have to learn a lot about responsibility. In the heart we can sit back and say, 'I can go to the base and I can deal with my fear, I can go to the sacral and deal with those sexual ages and creativity, I can go to the solar plexus I can deal with the anger issues, the hatred, the bitterness. I can deal with those sensations.' In the Heart Chakra we are in the centre of the see-saw. However, when we get to the Throat Chakra we have to take action, we have to speak it and express our feelings, our thoughts and then be responsible for them.

This is a wonderfully challenging chakra. The throat is the first of the higher spiritual centres – this is followed by the Brow and the Crown; the lower three are the personality, the Heart is in the middle position acting as a point of balance and conduit between them. Then you come up to the Throat and this is the spiritual centre where we acknowledge responsibility and our spirituality, and this is not an easy one. Our first responsibility is to authentically express our truth. Now remember that this is *our* truth, not somebody else's truth. We can go along with beautiful Teachings, with their wonderful wisdom and knowledge. We can reflect those in our belief system but is it our own truth? Have we realized those Teachings within ourselves? We have to understand what these beautiful teachers and Masters are giving us and at some level we can say, 'Yes I can go along with that' but going along and actually authenticating it in our lives is a different thing. What is the point of us following a teacher or Master if we're not going to be living that truth in our own lives? The teachers and Masters are moving and evolving all the time so their truths are changing. So, it has to be our Truth from our own experiences. Their truth served to teach us to realize Truth in our lives, and to move on. Each one of us has a different purpose, we don't lose ourselves we rather merge into the greater Self, but we never lose our individuality, instead we become at one with the Great Being.

It's about saying what we mean with kindness and compassion and with sincerity. It's about being mindful of where other people are and the need to be tolerant. It's about being tactful and kind in what we do and say.

Sometimes people can be so blunt, and they can be very hard. For some people it's way too strong. This can also be provocative and ends up creating the opposite effect. It puts peoples' backs up and they may shy away. It's a shame because they may have something lovely to offer but it's the way it's been expressed that's the problem. So it's about being very mindful about how we express ourselves, never deviating from our own truth because often, until we've learnt the lesson of the 5$^{th}$ Chakra, and we learn how to activate that in a positive way, we say things we think other people want to hear. This could be because we lack confidence in ourselves, we want to be popular with people and we don't want to cause any ripples along the way. There could many reasons why we act like this and this can also come from our own perceptions and indoctrination. This is all about the path of growth. We are all each other's teachers and students. I reiterate here what I have said in previous chapters – we need to get the balance of all these chakras, otherwise we are at the risk of raising the kundalini before we are ready.

Our speech reflects our fears and our feelings and that is why it is important to keep going back to the previous Chakras, so that we can balance them and transmute any negativity.

Remember in the previous Chakras, we've gone through the four elements related to each of those chakras, but now we are looking at the ether and, in a sense, this gives us a kind of matrix for our creativity, our dreams and hopes, our aspirations because we have been opening up all the other chakras along the journey. Our dreams and aspirations can be really creative here and take effect in this chakra, because we can voice and express them. Think too about how people with tremendous gifts and skills might find it difficult to express those in a teaching capacity because they have not yet worked through the lessons of this chakra. Developing this Chakra not only gives us the ability to be able to express our particular gift or skill but inspires others to greater things themselves. When we are able to express this, we are reaching out to their Heart Chakra, to their own Light. This is like the domino effect. As we express and share our truth, our Light with others, so others will also be inspired to share their own truth, their own Light.

All the chakras are beautiful because they all have their own relevance and significance, but I find when I get to the Throat Chakra it almost gives me a new platform. In this platform I can actually authenticate everything that I am. It's also a space, a time for introspection because we've been through all the experiences, the sensations, the feelings and the knowledge of the first four Chakras and now we have reached this platform where we can express them. How we express our Truth is of course very important. At this level, if we have not fully completed the previous Chakras then our indoctrination, our perceptions will dictate what we see as our Truth. So, we go back to the old question, what is my Truth? This is the dialogue that goes between us and the Observer, or the Silent Watcher.

What do I mean by the Observer or the Silent Watcher? The Observer is our Higher Self which is our spirit. At this level, we are aware that we are more than just the physical body. We are aware that we are also a Soul, a Spirit. The Observer is there to observe how our personality deals with our everyday encounters. The Observer, or the Silent Watcher, can also be called our Guardian Angel (or our Higher Self) that guides us through our experiences. This essence, this Being, is there to help us go through the experiences we have chosen for our soul lessons. It cannot and will not interfere with us because we've got free will. The Observer is detached from us whilst we are still in our personality. However, once we get to the 4$^{th}$ and 5$^{th}$ chakras we become more and more in tune with our Observer because we are growing spiritually. Our personality is still very necessary and it will continue its journey through life experiences until it has learned all the soul lessons of the chakras, raising the consciousness up, up and up. Once we get to the Crown Chakra we become one with the Observer.

It is worth remembering that with the Throat Chakra we can do much good, but we could also do harm. The negative aspect of this Chakra is the harm that we can do by continually gossiping. There are those who maliciously set out to destroy a person's reputation, therefore we need to be aware of karma here. It's not just about *how* we say something; we need to think *where* these words are coming from and where they are going.

Along the journey of the Soul evolving through the chakras we start identifying with the life around us and as we unfold the spiritual qualities, as we learn the lessons of each chakra, so we are spreading our vision and our perspective even further and we are more aware of things going on in our community and nation. When we get to the 5$^{th}$ chakra we begin to see a more global perspective. Our understanding is more global. Therefore, the experiences that we have encountered in life have hopefully made us a little wiser and we see things from a different perception.

Perhaps whilst we were still experiencing the lessons of the solar plexus, we might have been prejudiced about people, issues, cultures, but when we get to the 4$^{th}$ and 5$^{th}$ chakras we see things from a different perspective. We appreciate that it is through understanding other cultures that we grow. We are growing all the time and that's exactly what we should be doing if we are learning our lessons. However, this may not always be the case. If we refuse to accept the lessons, and we need to remember we have free will to choose whether we go one way or another, then we won't grow. We stay in a continuous round of lifetimes until eventually the penny drops.

It is very possible that we can get so caught up in the 2$^{nd}$ and 3$^{rd}$ chakras, that we remain trapped on the level of sensations and feelings and possibly fear, unable to free ourselves from them. This means that we are not open to wider perspectives. Therefore, we may stay in that closed environment of prejudice and bias, not caring a hoot about anyone else so long as 'we're alright Jack'. We can see the bias and prejudice going on in the world right now. Look around and notice what's going on, people being so bigoted in their attitudes and perceptions of life - they don't care what they say or do or about hurting others; what is dangerous about bigoted people is that they make statements, they express their bigotry in a such a forceful powerful way that it can flatten or destroy other people around them. That's why this is such a powerful Chakra which needs to be gently opened and fully understood.

## The root level of the Throat chakra

The throat means creativity but also introspection. The ability to go within, to help us to understand the fundamental issues of life. Therefore, the root of the throat relates to how we understand life around us and how we understand the bigger world around us because we want to express our views and our feelings about 'what's going on' and the throat chakra gives the root that opportunity to understand in order to express.

## The sacral level of the Throat chakra

We know that the sacral is about the sensations and the senses. So, when we get to the sacral of the throat we need to also understand and express the different senses that we feel. For example, what is this sensation about? How do I express what I am feeling? Have I balanced my sensations well enough so that I can express them in a loving, wise manner? The sacral in the throat is about how we express our sensations and senses.

## The solar plexus level of the Throat chakra

We know the solar plexus is about emotions. It's about our philosophy, our understanding, our family life, the philosophy of life through our emotions. The philosophy of life is about the joy of living. What does the joy of living mean to you? What is your anger? How do you express your anger? How do you express your joy, hatred, happiness, deep gratitude? It's how you express all those different emotions. All the time it is about learning. It is also about realizations of being. **This is who I am** and I want to express who I am. How I can best do this? At this level we want to understand our positive and good emotions and enjoy Being.

## The heart level of the Throat chakra

This is about the expressions of the heart and the heart of course is balance, it also brings us harmony. As we know, the Ray connected to this Chakra is the 4$^{th}$ which is Harmony through Conflict. At this level we have the opportunity to harmonize our heart in relation to the life we are living.

For example, the Heart Chakra may be open but if we are living in dire circumstances that is not so easy to do. How can we express what we are feeling in our hearts if we are in a relationship with someone who continuously moans and is negative about life? Someone who doesn't understand and belittles everything we say. Or we could be in a situation where we are having incredible problems with our children, friends, work etc. How do you express our heart in these kinds of circumstances?

When we are beautifully harmonized and balanced, we can rise above our circumstances and start thinking about the harmony of life itself. What's life about? What is the meaning of life? This is fine, of course, when we are enjoying harmonious conditions around us. But when we have conditions around us that are not harmonious, when we have a partner that maybe doesn't understand what we're talking about or agree with us, when we have problems with our children, or if we're in a job where other colleagues make it stressful and difficult, how do we harmonize ourselves? Much of this of course is to do with karma but remember we have, at Soul level, chosen that karma in order to transmute and learn from it. However, our purpose is to unfold those chakras within us. So, we need to transmute karma, learn the Soul lesson of this chakra and at the same time remember that we are being influenced by the Ray of this Chakra and the Initiation.

However tough and challenging as it may appear by the time we start developing this Chakra we have a glimpse of the spiritual path and this makes it much easier. We come back to balance and harmony. We also get our perspective into balance, acknowledging that our perceptions can be clouded by our indoctrination. Balance, balance, balance. We are told time and time again by the Masters that we cannot judge another. This is especially important on the spiritual path. We cannot, we dare not judge. For we truly do not know what another soul is going through and at what level.

It's about having that understanding and that compassion for the circumstances and situation that others find themselves in and not being judgmental. The heart brings us wonderful opportunities for harmonizing not just our own lives but helping to facilitate it in the lives of others.

## The throat of the Throat chakra

We know that the Throat Chakra is the Will to Express, the Will to speak and communicate our feelings, sensations and what we are. We have matured to an extent where we are a philosopher, maybe just to ourselves to start with, but we have become a philosopher of our lives. Therefore, the throat is about expressing our own philosophy or intuition. When we reach the throat level of the throat chakra we are more mature. This is now the soul speaking on a far deeper level, expressing itself, communicating and asking – who am I? What have I reached here? I've reached this platform, I've gone through these teachings and I really enjoyed that, but what do I believe? What am I going to express to people? Am I going to express only other Teachers? What are my own thoughts? What have I learnt?.

## The brow level of the Throat chakra

The Brow we know is concerned with perceptions. This is about what we perceive of our lives and how we express those perceptions. This can be incredibly positive or negative because if we haven't fully developed our other chakras our perceptions in life will be limited and biased. Consequently, we can only express where we are and our perceptions up to that point. If we have really balanced our heart centre and our other chakras, then our perception of life is going to be more balanced. Remember though perceptions are not just about our feelings, they are also about our thoughts.

Our perceptions are so significant particularly in this day and age. They are significant at any time but now because of social media we can get more information about what's happening in the world and how we perceive things. It is vital to remember that we need to perceive life from the viewpoint of the Soul and the Spirit. The danger here is that often we perceive life from the personality, with all its distorted opinions and views, based solely on our indoctrination and conditioning.

## The crown level of the Throat chakra

The Crown Chakra is the most spiritual, the highest we can attain in the physical body. Hence, when we get to the crown level in the throat chakra this brings us purity and enlightened expression. We have a measure of understanding and the benefit of the lessons of all the other chakras on the way up and it is expressed in a pure way. We have mentioned previously that we get to a point where we can be our own philosopher, the crown level in this chakra is in a sense that philosopher and brings us confirmation of who we are. When there are imbalances in the 5$^{th}$ Chakra you find people who often interrupt, and they have to keep on speaking - that's an imbalance in the throat chakra. Then there's the opposite. People who don't speak very much, who are probably very shy and don't like speaking in public about their views. This Chakra is about communication but it's also about creativity. They go beautifully together because the more open we are the more wonderful and varied expressions of creativity there are.

## Conclusion:

Most people use their voice almost exclusively to communicate the emotional needs of their lower chakras. As we become conscious of our psychological and spiritual resources, the 5$^{th}$ Chakra grows in strength as we discover our own truth. With the help of the lessons of harmony from the Heart chakra, in this chakra we have found the ability to voice and to express our truth in a caring and tactful manner.

# The Sixth Chakra is the Brow

**The Will to See**

> **Influences & Links:**
>
> Colour is Indigo (see Chapter 6 for more explanation on the colour)
>
> Planet is Uranus
> Uranus is the planet that can hit us like a flash of lightning. There are times when we may suddenly get that illumination, that inspiration that gives us the answer we have been seeking.
>
> Element is Light
> This is truly about enlightenment. When we have unfolded this Chakra to its fullest degree, we will have clarity. This Light contributes to our understanding, our perception, intuition, imagination.
>
> Soul Lesson
> Our lesson here is to rise above our conditioned perceptions and see Truth. We can then Walk our truth, Be our truth.
>
> Possible physical problems
> Eyesight, glaucoma, cataracts, macular degeneration. Brain, tumours, haemorrhages, strokes. Itchy eyes, seizures, epilepsy. Depression and anxiety attacks.

## The 6th Chakra – the Brow - Pituitary

The 6th Chakra is the Brow, the Pituitary gland. Also known as the Third Eye. Although the colour associated with this Chakra is Indigo you can see also hints of blue and amethyst. It's almost as though it's combining the throat, the heart and the actual crown in that one colour.

The 6th Chakra is about the Will to See. It's also about perceptions, intuition and imagination. The Crown and the Brow are connected to the Root Chakra. Although we receive the full enlightenment of the I AM in the Crown we begin to perceive something of this aspect when we get to the Brow. The connection is with the 6th Ray of Devotion and Idealism. The element is Light (seeing clearly). The planet is Uranus, the planet that can hit us like lightning sometimes. It brings us a flash of vision and clarity. This is the Chakra that, in a sense, helps us to integrate the inner leadership with the personality.

We begin to take stock. We have gone through the personality chakras and with the Brow we can perceive and integrate how the three lower chakras have helped in our unfoldment, in our development. We are able to understand more clearly where we are today and how we got there; why we had to take all those stepping stones in the past and along the journey; this is truly about perception. We know that perception means we can see clearly but we also know that perception can come from our own indoctrination and can cloud our judgment; it can cloud how we see things. There are, therefore, two aspects of this Chakra. Until we have balanced these two aspects properly, in other words until we've opened the Third Eye we cannot really see with clear vision what is happening, neither can we see where we are and what the journey is all about. Until we attain that clarity, perception can delude us because it comes from our conditioning and indoctrination. In other words, the Higher Mind needs to be prepared and made ready before the Higher Consciousness can enter in. It's down to us to train ourselves in pure thinking, pure living to help us be ready to receive the incoming of this wonderful Divine illumination and enlightenment.

This is how we achieve the vision, the truth in our thoughts and emotional astuteness. We need to transmute and rise above our negative perceptions, our indoctrination, our habitual thinking and old belief systems. Until we do that we cannot be ready for the incoming of that pure Light, that Higher Consciousness. The emotional astuteness is bringing the solar plexus to the heart and those are the positive emotions, positive feelings not the imbalances nor all the negativity. When the Third Eye is activated in a positive and balanced way it is the instrument for our psychic awareness - higher intuitive clairvoyance can come, because we are perceiving or receiving clearly from other worlds, it's not just this two-dimensional world. We are seeing the stepping stones beyond death, beyond the physical.

It's also creative. As we can see from experiencing and developing the Chakras all the colours fuse as we begin to balance them. In the Throat Chakra (5th) we are creating but in the 6th Chakra we are actually perceiving our creation and taking it further. If we don't balance this, if we are still conditioned, our creativity is going to be limited or compromised by the past and what we have unfolded in ourselves. This means that all these chakras are limited to our present state of where we are. This is why the 6th Chakra is so wonderful because our lives are about perception. The more we go through our lives, the more we can see how we can suddenly react to a train of thought or to something being said. Then afterwards, we can look back and think, 'Why did I react like that? Where did my thoughts come from, were they mine? Or am I reacting this way because that's how I've been conditioned for the past x years. That's why this Chakra is so beautiful and so powerful because it opens us up for the higher consciousness.

This is the Chakra that the sages of old, and the seers of the world can see beyond and bring a different perception to reality, or what we consider as reality. Often a seed is planted, we may have a new train of thought and perhaps at first it appears a bit extreme to the majority of people, but perhaps it has reached one or two people in the room. Something has connected, possibly for the future. The Brow is another bridge (Antahkarana). When we open up that Third Eye, when our perceptions are clear, beautiful insights can come in and then we open up that bridge which is a clearer path to our higher consciousness. We don't consciously open it; this happens naturally as we unfold, clear our perceptions and our vision because the soul is ready for that to happen.

The Brow Chakra is the highest idealism, We're talking about the 6th Ray of Devotion and Idealism and this is the highest idealism. The 6th Ray is connected with the Piscean Age, with so much indoctrination and fanaticism etc. But there is also the idealism in its highest form and our aspiration towards that idealism which involves our intuition and imagination. The 6th Ray is also about devotion. Our devotion to idealism is not to a guru, or a teacher, or a belief system, it's a devotion to a higher ideal. However, the personality needs a form, and this may come in the form of a teacher, a guru, a dogma, doctrines, or teachings. When we get to the 6th Chakra there's no personality involved, there's no form, it's an ideal, it's abstract.

The chakra for the Brow is located in the middle of the forehead and it's also in Hindu tradition the Third Eye of Shiva. Shiva grants knowledge and truth, perfect truth and non-duality. It's the Oneness. So the ideal is the Oneness. From this Chakra we also learn that we are not separate from God or the Highest. We are One and part of the Whole, because that's where the clarity and the vision exists. This is our authentic Self. If we've got that clearer vision, if we can see beyond, we can see Truth, non-duality, non-attachment to anything; this then is truly our authentic Self. It's what we're all aiming for –one day!

One of the lessons of this Chakra is to learn to discern or understand the difference between gathering factual information and real knowledge. Anybody can gather information nowadays, anyone can get on to Google and get information about anything, a stream of facts and figures. We are not attached to that information other than our minds because that's all it is, it's just information. If we thrive on information it can make us feel good. We can sit and quote this and that and that's great but it's simply information about facts. It's not knowledge that has been gained through experience. Experience comes from living our life, coping with our challenges, rising above the dross to see a higher ideal. Real knowledge is what we have learned and experienced from life. When we can say 'I know that I am, I know this is it because I have experienced it and this is my truth and I have realized that truth within myself.' That's knowledge! Otherwise it's just information. There's nothing wrong with that. By gathering information we can understand that there's more to life and it serves a purpose. But it has limitations and it is important to understand that. Information on any subject can make for interesting discussions, it can be helpful to other people – 'Oh I never knew that' and this can set them off on another train of thought or exploration. Nothing is wasted - it's a question of levels. There's nothing wrong with gathering information but when we get to the 6th Chakra it's knowledge that's been obtained by our own experiences. So that's the difference and clarity come with that.

This Chakra helps us because as we unfold that higher consciousness it influences the physical mind. It could be said that this chakra acts as a clearing house and we are working towards clearing old conditioning, perceptions or karma, our way of thinking in the past, anything we have retained from the past that is still affecting us currently. This is all part of the clearing house of the 6th Chakra.

I repeat that, in this Chakra, we are clearing the way for the higher consciousness and this does not necessarily mean an easy time. This is the chakra that says, 'Thus far'! It acts as a gateway and we need to clear old perceptions before we can move on. If this Chakra is too open we could spend our days dreaming, we may not be able to focus on anything in particular. It is possible that we experience anxiety attacks, mental anxiety attacks, panic attacks and although we relate that to the personality remember that the Brow is connected to the Root Chakra and that is the connection. Our mental bodies may have very deep-rooted fears that can create panic/anxiety attacks. Other conditions may also be depression, confusion, poor judgment because we lack the confidence to judge anything and indecisiveness because we don't trust ourselves. There may be mental blockages when we point blankly refuse to accept something. 'I don't want to know that'. Probably there's fear at the root (base) of it but it's coming from a wish not to see something.

## **The root level of the Brow chakra**

The Root Chakra is about fear, instinct, survival- so how is this going to affect the root of the Brow? If, by the time we get to the Brow, we haven't completely balanced the Root Chakra, it could cloud our vision. We wouldn't be able to see or think clearly and, if we did, it would probably be distorted. There would need to be enough consciousness and perception to understand where that distortion came from and also how we can deal with it. Remember that because the Root is instinctive and the Brow is about Intuition and perception, in a way, there is potential conflict. However, the fact that we have reached the level of the Brow Chakra will help us to understand if our initial instinct is based on fear or self-preservation. In our developing the Brow Chakra we can get some clarity about our fears.

At this level, we have risen through the Chakra and we are not at the root of the root where we have little experience or knowledge. We've gone up the chakras, we've already obtained some knowledge and wisdom so when we get to the 6th our intuition is going to say to our instinct, 'Hang on a minute, we know about self-preservation, we absolutely concur about the instinctual apprehension we may have', (because by this point it's not so much fear as apprehension about doing or knowing something). So that deep-rooted fear has been tempered and our 6th Chakra is saying 'Let's bring clarity to this.'

## **The sacral level of the Brow chakra**

Through the unfolding and working through the soul lessons of this Chakra we are dealing with imbalances or parts of ourselves that we need to cleanse and clear. Sensations, people, relationships, so how do we deal with that in our lives when we get to the Brow? At this point, it may serve us to pause. Sensations can be unreliable, ill informed, they might be bang on the mark or not, so discernment and discrimination are helpful. Sensations are not reliable, but they are part of our experiences. In the Brow, the 6th Chakra, we begin to **see** how our sensations can be adapted and balanced. All the time the 6th Chakra is teaching clarity, balance etc. and bringing intuition and new perceptions to our understanding which in turn brings confidence and is very enabling. Also, by doing this our relationships with people change because we are seeing them in a different way. We are able to influence and change our perceptions and our reactions to people. Seeing things in a different way is the beauty of this Chakra.

## **The solar plexus of the Brow chakra**

This level is about our emotions, good and negative which can be all over the place. How do we perceive those? It's the same principle. Where does our anger come from? Remember the knowledge derived from our experiences (not information) that we have within us and that we are wise enough now to say 'Hang on a minute, what are we getting angry and upset about? Why do we dislike that person?' If there is no reason where is it coming from? At this level the opportunity is there for our intuition to guide us into expressing and managing our emotions in a more positive way. We don't 'control' our emotions, we can 'manage' our emotions in a better way because we have more understanding.

We have gone through the Heart Chakra with the love and mercy and compassion so what the 6th Chakra does is it enables us to use the knowledge that we have gained in unfolding our Heart Chakra to bring that into our solar plexus, our sacral and root and manage and enable these chakras to function in a more beautiful, positive and balanced way. What we are doing all the time is spiritualizing all the chakras. Our creativity, our feelings and our instincts are all part of us, and we could not be a fully unfolded Spiritual being until we've been able to touch the Root and that's why the Crown and the Brow Chakras are connected to the Root.

## The heart level of the Brow chakra

At this level, the heart is unfolding with compassion and unconditional love, with generosity and grace and our 6th chakra is perceiving the beauty. We perceive our qualities as beautiful gifts and we live our lives with these beautiful gifts and use them to serve others. We perceive, we see things and life and people from a very different perception. A perception based on love and understanding.

## The throat level of the Brow chakra

At the Throat level of this Chakra we are expressing our creativity, we are speaking our truth from a higher perspective. Just think how wonderful it is that we can speak our truth with the clarity of the 6th Chakra. We are coming from our authentic self and we are able to express our truth. So many beautiful Teachers have done this because they have unfolded and balanced their Chakras and they're able to express their truths. When we speak from our truth we will be heard. Others may not agree but they will hear and sometimes situations that could have been very awkward or difficult can go down a different route because Truth has its own resonance with the hearts of others. Think how much we can help people with the opening of the heart expressing our truth, our creativity and our perception. We are seeing things in a different light. Think what wonderful knowledge we can share with others.

## The brow level of the Brow chakra

At this level, we are coming from clear thinking, clarity, open and expressive creativity and we are also clearing the pathway, not just from this lifetime but from others because we are preparing ourselves for the opening of the Crown Chakra.

## The crown level of the Brow chakra

This is the spiritual 'knowing' not the personality thinking it knows. This is what gives us a clearer vision, this is what our Soul is aiming for. The spiritual 'knowing' is knowing what it needs to clear from its perception and change our thinking to a higher perspective. It's that simple.

## Conclusion:

This is a highly sensitive chakra. As we aspire to the highest, the Crown, we are preparing ourselves for higher and better forms of life. The creative intention of the 5th Chakra is focused here and may be considered the centre of the highest idealism. This then becomes the agent of the Soul when the Soul is fully dominating the personality after the 3rd Initiation.

# The Seventh Chakra is the Crown
(top of the head)

**I Know That I Am - The Will to Be**

**Influences & Links:**

Colour is Violet and Gold (see Chapter 6 for more explanation on the colour)

Planets are Sun/Neptune
The Sun is the life force. Neptune, ruler of the oceans (water) carries the life aspect to every part of the body.

Element is Thought, Wisdom, Spiritual Connection

Soul Lesson
This is the Will to Be, the *I Know that I Am*. When the Soul has completed all the seven levels and reached full consciousness, its only remaining desire is to serve all life.

Possible physical problems:
Crown energy centre – Spirit, Will, Openness, Values, Ethics, Courage, Faith and Inspiration. Anxiety, depression anything that involves the upper head. Bi polar, anyone with amnesia or is in a coma- they're trying to find that balance there, the usual headaches and really big migraines, epilepsy, brain tumours, strokes, dementia, Alzheimer's, MS, Motor Neuron disease, Parkinson's, anything that's affected because of the brain. Any mental illness, e.g. OCD, schizophrenia or ADHD.

## **The Seventh Chakra is The Crown - Pineal**

This Chakra is about 'I know' and the 'Will to Be'. In other words, the I AM at the Higher Consciousness It is literally just Being, being the I AM. I know that I AM, it's the Presence, it's the Oneness, the Higher Consciousness. There are so many words that we can give to it. The Crown Chakra is influenced by the 7$^{th}$ Ray which we know is the Ray of Ritual, Ceremony, Law and Order. The Colour is violet – with gold. Gold is the colour of the Higher Consciousness and Light and of course the gold also represents enlightenment. The planets are the Sun and Neptune.

This is the Chakra of wisdom, of knowledge and of spiritual connection, not just in relation to the body but on the higher levels, stepping beyond. It's the energy centre, the Spirit, the Will, the Oneness, it's all our spiritual ethics, values, qualities, everything. Think of all the spiritual qualities of courage, strength and faith, This is the energy centre that fuses all our qualities together as One. The Crown Chakra is particularly connected to the human soul and world service because once we have reached that higher level of understanding – and this is connected to the Initiations as well- we come back in service or at least the opportunity is there to continue to serve on Earth. Some Masters, or Higher Beings, also choose to serve in other areas of the planetary system.

Both the pineal and the pituitary gland (Brow and Crown) are closely associated with the Root, the base of the spine. We know that the fires of life, the Kundalini, reside at the Root and only with the unfoldment and the balancing of each chakra can this Divine Fire with its creative urge, rise up the spine from the Root to the Crown.

By this time, the soul infused personality brings up (from the Kundalini) the fires right through the spine right up to the very top. Think of all our instincts, our sensations, our feelings, our heart, our compassion, our love, our expression, our truth and our perception. It is all aligned at the very top. It is all one. Then we are ready to serve and to *be* and by the time that wonderful illumination and enlightenment happens, we are no longer limited to the earth karma, we've gone through our karma. This is why the clearing house of the 6$^{th}$ chakra (the Brow) is so important. We've gone through that, we've got a clear pathway to serve. From now on we are serving from the highest ideal.

There are imbalances until we develop the Crown and this is all about taking inner leadership. It is the Higher Self that is now in charge. It is our Higher Self, our Spirit, which takes the responsibility. There's no longer a personality when you get to the Crown of the Crown. With this responsibility comes the surrender of the personality. This may entail us going through some real physical problems, we can only imagine what we have got to clear before we can reach that.

The Crown Chakra is the summit, the crowning achievement. This is the distributing agent of the Will energy of God, the 1st Ray. The distributing agents are the 1st and the 7th Rays. They are both connected as Will energy proceeds downward from the spiritual tree of the Monad, through the Antahkarana and provides the Initiate, the Adept, the Master with the power to accomplish the purpose of Shambala, and Shambala is the seat of the Masters. This is the purpose of the role of Shambala on earth, the raising of our consciousness to the Highest; this means the 1st and the 7th Rays working together. What we are doing is literally implementing the Will of Shambala on earth. This is the knowledge and purpose of the Masters of Wisdom. We need to get to that top Initiation before we can understand what the Will and Purpose of Shambala is.

Divine Will encounters no hindrance or obstruction and this centre is its radiating dynamo into the world of man. This is the centre which relates the Initiate to the Master Teachers, to the Council of Shambala and to the Lord of the World, Sanat Kumara. The 6th and 7th chakras together produce an electromagnetic field and when stimulated they bring about union. They create the intense light in the head that radiates outwardly and is often depicted in paintings of enlightened Souls and called 'halos' by Christian seers and adepts. That's the Crown of the Crown. It's worth remembering that the 6th Ray is the Ray of the Mystic, the 7th Ray is the Ray of the Practical Mystic. This means that we are bringing back everything that we have learnt, knowledge gained and we're bringing it back to serve in a practical way, to ground it.

The lesson of the 7th Chakra, is Mastery of Time. Linear time is no longer needed. We use linear time because we have to. The Masters will use linear time when they're back here to serve. But when we become a Master, or a Higher Initiate we become Masters of Time. Linear time, as we know it, doesn't exist for them. We break free of linear time; we're no longer in a tyrannical grip of the body, of the earth or of the past because we've cleared that karma. This is where the Masters are free to work wherever they need to. They have no concept of time as we have, they have mastered time so therefore they can come and go, appear or disappear, because for them time is nothing and also because they're not held back by karma. Their bodies of Light are free.

In the 7th Chakra we acquire knowledge of the past and future. We're still dealing with the past, we're healing it and that's why so many of us are here today - we are healers because we're healing our past. That's what the 7th Chakra enables us to do. What we also learn in this Crown Chakra is that life is like a tapestry and there are lines of threads that we take from the past. That is how we influence our future by taking the past, changing ourselves and so we influence the future. Life is the pattern in the intricate web of a tapestry that we can use to create this pathway.

Now a negative expression of the 7th Chakra could be spiritual regression. If we have not unfolded the other chakras to a good level, to a balanced level; if we're perceiving spirituality from an unclear perception, that is almost like a regression. We need to go back to the chakras and cleanse and clear whatever is necessary because otherwise we cannot move on. This is not about being negative; it is rather the soul's journey and it's only known as a regression because we've got to step back to heal what still needs attention. We're simply going back to put things right.

There's also something worth remembering here, just because we reach the Crown chakra doesn't mean we know it all. We may have an awareness of the spirit and presence within, but it is only after the 4th Initiation that we truly realise and know this. There are other Initiations, and we only know of the Initiations that affect our path on earth. It is worth remembering that just because we have unfolded some of the Crown Chakra we don't know it all. There's still a little ego left in the personality and while that ego may not be negative it may reach a point where we think, 'Wow I know I am Spirit and it could, in some cases, lead to arrogance. However, once we have reached the 4th Initiation we let go of all that. We continue to evolve. We are only on planet earth and we are only in one planetary system, we have little information on the solar system, and we know even less about the cosmos or the galaxies beyond that. Even the Masters don't know everything. So, it's beyond our limited understanding.

Another hazard on the path stems from ignorance and pride where those people who have a tiny bit of spiritual knowledge think they have attained a great deal; the peril here then is that they can influence others. There are risks in believing that we know it all, discrimination again! We need that balance of feet on the ground, head in the heavens. Above all, we need that wonderful spiritual quality of Humility.

We understand the difference between the outer forms and that which is formless. It's like seeing the river flowing and the water running through our fingers. This is the influence of Neptune. This is what we attain when we have properly balanced the Crown Chakra.

If we are overly open in the Crown chakra there could be a tendency to be a bit airy fairy about life. Then of course our physical health can suffer because there's a lack of focus. The other interesting thing about the Crown Chakra is that it doesn't mean that only people with spiritual beliefs can unfold fully in that Chakra. An atheist can unfold that Chakra- they don't have a dogma and perhaps see life from a very different perspective, without indoctrination of orthodoxy.

## **The root level of the Crown chakra**

When we get to the Crown chakra, this is when we start getting interested in mysterious things. Perhaps something that's mysterious that we've never tackled before because our indoctrination, conditioning or perception have made that difficult. Some people get involved with cults or organisations that appear to have a mystical air about them. There are those who have a yearning for knowledge of the mysterious – and that can cover a wide range of groups or organisations. Therefore, this is where we need to have unfolded the wonderful spiritual qualities of Discrimination and Discernment.

## **The sacral level of the Crown chakra**

At this level we are beginning to spiritualize our life, therefore we shall be seeing other people differently; our relationships with other people will be different. We're beginning to understand our sensations, our lives, our relationships in a different way. So, it's like spiritualizing our relationship with others and also with our own life. As we understand our sensations, desires and feelings, we elevate them to a higher level. We live in harmony with our inner self, and accept life and its many challenges with a more balanced attitude.

## The solar plexus level of the Crown chakra

Because the solar plexus level is that of our emotions when we reach the Crown Chakra, we begin to balance these emotions, or rather the opportunities are there for us to attain that balance. We search for someone on our level of understanding rather than on the physical level only. At this level, we see beyond the physical and we have that clarity, that deeper awareness to look at relationships differently. In other words, we begin to understand the beauty of another's soul, rather than just being impressed or unimpressed by the physical.

## The heart level of the Crown chakra

At this level, we see and know that the heart is full of compassion. We see the grace, the loving, the caring, the understanding and the wisdom, all that we are bringing into our lives. What we are doing is bringing all that knowledge of who we are, harmonising the spiritual qualities within our heart centre together with discrimination, detachment, discernment and common sense.

## The throat level of the Crown chakra

At this level what we are expressing is our truth, our knowledge and our creativity in a far more authentic way. When we listen to teachers of Wisdom we can resonate with them from our own understanding and experience. By this time, we have rooted out all that is no longer of service to us, we have balanced our sensations and emotions, we have opened our hearts in love, compassion and wisdom, and now we have the opportunity to express all these.

## The brow level of the Crown chakra

Our reality, our vision and our intuition is coming from the highest level. It's another world. We are seeing things from another world; our clairvoyance is of the highest order. It's not of the psychic astral level which is caught up with our emotions and fears, it's altogether of a greater calibre. At this point our intuition is clear as it's coming from the I AM. Also, our perception of life is clearer because we are perceiving everything from a spiritual angle all the time.

## The crown level of the Crown chakra

At this level, the Crown of the Crown Chakra is our teacher of the highest wisdom, it's as simple as that. There's nothing more that can be said. When we get there we have attained full Consciousness. Because most of us, in the earthly physical body, haven't got there yet we can only imagine what it could be. But at this level, we know there is more, the greater beyond.

## Conclusion:

This is our crowning achievement. This Chakra is connected to service as the developing human Soul and is related to the atmic level. Souls who master the gifts of this chakra understand that the river of life flows beyond form and formlessness, beyond existence and nonexistence. They know infinity independent of time or form.

# CHAPTER 8

# Where does karma fit into all this?

In our matrix is the memory of all our past lives, some more significant than others. Our journey through the Chakras enables us to walk back through the doorway of past lives and learn how to face, understand and transmute karma or learn unfinished lessons.

Since all lives are connected by a thread, a link, it is the most important lives that have had the greatest impact in our unfoldment and evolution. It is these that we need to face. We need to remember that karma is not a punishment but rather a wonderful opportunity to learn from the past, and free ourselves from the heavy baggage that we have carried over many lifetimes.

We can transmute karma by accepting and by our understanding of those experiences which have imprisoned us. Karma does not necessarily have to wait several lifetimes to be discharged. It can happen within a few hours or it can happen in a lifetime.

Karma is the law of cause and effect – an unbreakable law of the cosmos. Our actions create our future. Our fate is never sealed because we have freewill.

*Every act creates Karma by our desire, thought and action.*

How do we begin to understand what karma is and how can we transmute this?

- By accepting that our lives are continuous
- By accepting that our responsibilities evolve from one lifetime to another
- By studying the Laws of Karma
- Negative karma is created by an absence of wisdom – through ignorance by an unevolved soul
- By the recognition that we are far greater than the little self in this one life and that therefore our journey is connected to the whole of humanity's evolution through the Ages, Cycles, Rounds, Root-races
- By the understanding and knowledge that through past lives experiences, we have traversed the Earth, sometimes falling, picking ourselves up but continuously evolving
- By the awareness of the inter-connection with all life around us. All the kingdoms of nature, mineral, vegetable, animal – all is within us
- By recognising that we need to understand and work with the Elements around and within us
- By understanding that through meditation we are able at any time to go back and look at past lives, and heal our original wound
- **By recognising that the very essence, the very energy force that moves the Universe, is also within us**

Karma is something that we all experience. It is something we don't escape. Karma is absolutely the opportunity to learn and grow over many lives depending on the circumstances and how we react to the circumstances we find ourselves in. We bring it over from past lives. We create karma by our desires, our thoughts and our actions and each lifetime we accumulate karma. It is important to remember that not all karma is bad. We tend to think of karma as a punishment and it's not, it's an opportunity to learn.

If we were all wise and sages we would not be here would we? Life is about being and experiencing the normal circumstances in life. The Masters say that karma is a condition of the choices we make right now. We choose how we react to circumstances and conditions, everything we say and everything we think. We can't get away with anything just because nobody else can see it. We don't have a decided fate; we can change this at any moment. We are creating what's going to happen all the time and learning all the time. We are connected to everything in life, the cosmos and also ourselves past, present and future, physically, mentally and spiritually.

Desire, thought and action are the three main experiences that we put into operation when we react to circumstances. So how can we transmute karma? I know this is a big question – how do we do this?

## **By following and living the Twelve Great Laws of Karma**

1. <u>The Great Law of Cause and Effect</u> – The umbrella for all the laws- as you sow so shall you reap.

2. <u>The Law of Creation</u> - What we desire we create, contributing to a future for ourselves. We are creating all the time, and this governs what's going to happen to us. But while we are creating our karma we are also creating opportunities to learn our soul lessons.

3. <u>The Law of Connection</u> - We are connected to everything in life, the elements, the other kingdoms of nature and everything in the universe. The spark of life is in each one of us, the animal, vegetable and mineral kingdoms and throughout the cosmos itself. When we feel disconnected that's when our problems start because we have somehow cut ourselves off from all life.

4. <u>The Law of Responsibility</u> –Taking responsibility for ourselves, for everything that happens to us; we cannot blame our problems on anyone else; at the end of the day we are the only ones who are responsible for our actions. When things happen to us or when we see things happening outside it's so easy to say 'it must be karma' and we could sit back and not take any responsibility; but we are all responsible for everything that has/is happening in the world today whether it's by action or inaction. The Law of Responsibility

is there to make us see that we are part of a living creation of the One Spirit. We cannot say 'What's happening on the other side of the world is nothing to do with me' because at some point we are responsible because we all vibrate to the same note.

Karma that we create and immediately realize that we are wrong can be healed in that very moment by the recognition in our hearts that we have done wrong and by sincere penitence and contrition. It heals the karma instantly. It won't catch up with you in five lifetimes or whatever; it is dealt with in that moment of realization and contrition. We build up what I call debits and credits and it's only when the soul is strong enough that it can choose the best lifetimes in which to tackle difficult or outstanding karma. We can transmute some of our debits. Equally we may have gone through eons of lifetimes and we've really built up a lot of credits; we can choose a life for some experiences, but we don't have to pay off any debits. We see some people apparently waltzing through life where nothing seems to be happening to them, nothing seems to go wrong for them so maybe they're just using up all or some of their credits. This is why we have been told by the Masters again and again 'Do not judge.' We cannot judge because we cannot know the circumstances of everyone.

5. <u>The Law of Growth-</u> We have to put our own spiritual growth above so much. We have to grow spiritually and maybe make decisions that are hard for other people. We cannot control other people's lives; we can only control our own. It is we who must change our attitudes and reactions to other people, not those around us. If this doesn't work, rather than remain in a situation which could make us ill, or very unhappy, it is wiser to walk away, recognizing that the lessons to be learnt from this experience may have to be learnt at a later date. It takes strength and wisdom to make such a decision.

6. <u>The Law of Humility-</u> This is there to help us accept what there is, for what it is. Being in denial does not change what there is.

Having the humility to accept that 'OK I may not have done anything this lifetime to merit what's happened to me or someone I love' but it's very possible that from a previous lifetime something is owing and I need to repay this. Accepting doesn't mean giving up, it means that we realize that whatever has happened to us is a wonderful opportunity for our soul to learn and grow from that experience because we can inflict more hurt on ourselves by our negative reactions to what is happening to us. We have to accept and take full responsibility for our reactions.

7. <u>The Law of Focus-</u> We may think this is just focusing on what we're doing. This law also involves the focus on our lives, where we're going and what our aim is in life. It's not about being destructive in that focus. Let's say the soul has chosen in this life to learn the lesson of patience and we may have reached a point where we're saying, 'Oh I've had enough of all that, I'm patient all the time, nothing seems to change.' So, we lose our focus because any quality that we have to learn takes time. Spiritual qualities need to be learned on all the subtler bodies, i.e. physical, emotional, mental and spiritual. There's no hurry in the spiritual life. There is no time in Spirit. This law does not consider just this lifetime; it is focused on the path of the soul throughout many lifetimes.

8. <u>The Law of Hospitality and Giving</u>. It's the law of doing something for others without any selfish motive. It's the law of selflessness, of charitable giving for the right reasons, not because it's going to earn us some credits in the karmic field or kudos with others. It's got to come from the right motive of the heart. It shows our true intention and reveals that we are coming from the heart not the mind.

9. <u>The Law of Change</u>. People often say, 'Why do these things keep happening to me?' Because we're not learning from it, history continues to repeat itself unless we are willing to change. It's changing our desires, our sensations and feelings, our thoughts, and our actions. All of us from the moment we are born we are

indoctrinated and conditioned and it's jolly hard even to realize that the reason why history keeps repeating itself is because we're still living under those perceptions and indoctrination. Change is about knowing ourselves, being willing to let go and moving on. Self-knowledge is so important. We need to know ourselves, not the indoctrinated conditioned we that life has made us, but rather who we really are at soul level.

10. <u>The Law of the Here and Now.</u> The present is all there is. It's the here and now, what we are perceiving now, what we are thinking and desiring now is what makes our future. So it's no good thinking 'Oh well I'll be alright, I'll work on that in about five years' time and I'll be different' - well we won't be different if we haven't changed what we're thinking now. This is a wonderful Law.

11. <u>The Law of Patience.</u> Nothing of value is really created unless we have the patient mindset to evolve. We often speak of patience on the physical level, mental and emotional levels but one of our greatest challenges is spiritual patience especially when we start getting the awakening into the spiritual life. We want to get there fast and learn all there is to learn right now. We can go out there and chase so many different avenues of learning because our minds want to know all these things. If we follow the Law of Patience and we really knew ourselves, we would understand that our soul will bring to us those opportunities that we need and we don't have to chase here, there and everywhere. That doesn't mean we just sit back and do nothing. But when we are open and receptive to who we really are our soul will drop little jewels into our minds. Awareness will come, a book will drop into our hands and we will think 'Oh yes!' so it's having the patience of the spirit and realizing that what is right will come to us.

12. <u>The Law of Significance and Inspiration</u>. This is when we are in that 'trueness' with ourselves about the significance of life, the universal life. We understand the law of the universal life and that all life is one. When we understand that, that's when

our inspiration will come so that we can do what we need to do whatever that may be in order to help all life evolve. The crisis that is going on in humanity now is because humanity is evolving at a speed which is catching many people unawares and the chaos and the conflict is because we are dealing with past karma and opportunities for growth.

When we're trying to deal with all these things, all the chaos and conflict in life, the role for those who have a little bit of understanding is to really hold things steady by working with the Light and not to get ourselves in a state about life itself. We also need to try and understand as much as we can and not get depressed about the chaos and conflict in the world. That is just an outworking of karma; it's also working towards an opportunity for change in the Ages but also in the evolution of humanity. Humanity and the earth planet is evolving so, however chaotic and desperate things appear to be, we have a responsibility – the Law of Responsibility- to hold our Light steady. The Cosmos needs the Light because all the things that are going on produce darkness and we need as much Light as possible to balance the darkness.

## **By accepting reincarnation**

Our soul, the person we are, is an accumulation of all that we have been in other life times. We are the sum total of all the experiences, all the Soul lessons we have gone through and learned. We can therefore transmute karma because our karma in this lifetime is not just of this lifetime it's an accumulation of past lives.

## **By recognizing our connectedness.**

This is one of the Laws. Our connection is with all life but also our connection with ourselves, the past, the present and the future. All life is here, now and it's understanding the connection of all our lives but also recognizing the connection between our physical, our soul and our spirit. We are more than what we see right here, right now. What we see is the personality which is made up of our thoughts, our feelings and our physical body and those are connected to our lower chakras. The heart is the balance of everything. Then going up through the chakras, we have our higher spiritual Self. We're all aiming to transmute our karma, raise our consciousness from the root upwards and upwards until we get into our spiritual being. It is about recognizing that connection within ourselves, because if we can't connect with ourselves, if we don't understand ourselves, if we don't accept who we are, how can we accept another? When you have issues with other people, we need to ask ourselves, 'Where are they coming from?' Their personality more than likely; it's usually people reacting to situations from past conditioning or indoctrination or circumstances in their lives.

If we have an issue with someone where we have to respond or react, it's helpful if we try to do it in a way that puts it in the third person, ie: not 'What you've done or what you've said is wrong' but rather 'I have some problems with what has been said', 'I found what was said difficult'. By saying what we feel in this way, we take the sting away from direct confrontation. We need to acknowledge also that the other person is coming from past conditioning, thoughts, feelings and sensations. Soul understanding is soul healing. When we start understanding ourselves, we start understanding others. This is what brings healing.

Let's not let issues get to us. We need to take some responsibility for the fact that other people's actions are affected by what's going on for them and we can call a halt to this by understanding and not carrying the issue forward.

Humanity is evolving through the 1st, 2nd and 3rd Chakras, the sensations, the feelings etc but also, the opportunity is there for us to move on to the higher chakras and to express ourselves. This is the lesson which comes from the 5th Chakra- the throat- so the Soul/Spirit uses all the chakras in order to unfold. Therefore, whatever is going on in relation to our sensations and feelings being expressed through the throat, we do have to take responsibility for how we say things, how we do things. It is like a button that is being pressed so people can react to whatever it is.

There's something else here; the media, for all its fake news, does have a part to play in helping us to evolve. This is because the media can put out ideas that help us to discern what is truth and what is not. If there is still a streak of cruelty, of bullying or bias in someone it will eventually be expressed as this is the only way that it can be cleansed and healed. Sometimes when it is expressed, and it becomes OTT that's when people can look at it and say 'That's really gone too far now. I don't like this anymore.' That's when we start learning to discern and we can learn from all this.

If we go back to principles, ethics and values how can we take this forward? It seems now that all this has become lost- not forever- but just been put to one side. The blame culture we see is because nobody is taking responsibility. So, everything that's happening appears negative but it's truly a great opportunity for feelings to come to the surface and be released. That doesn't mean that in five years' time it'll all be over because people will learn at their own pace.

## **By understanding that every act creates karma.**

Karma comes from every desire, thought and action. Let's take desire first. You wish for something, whatever that may be and then our thoughts take it up – 'How can I do this, how can I get this? Then the actions happen because we then act upon it. If it's a wonderful thing, something positive and good that's great but if it's not…. For example, take the story of the slave wanting to murder the overseer because of his cruel behaviour - how can he do this? In all probability, the slave would be unable to do this because of the situation he's in that lifetime. However, if he should meet him in a future life, at soul level, there could be a strong recognition of antipathy. The Law of Karma says that if the intention behind our desire and our thought is very deep and strong, the action will take place. We may not, in this lifetime, flog him or punch him, but we may kick his car or suchlike. However, we are talking about transmuting karma. It is to be hoped that we will have then reached a place in our own soul development where we could think 'I really don't like that person', but there would not be a strong desire to do him harm. So, we let go of the intention because we don't want to hurt the other person. We may not realise it, but this is how we can transmute karma.

The karma has been balanced. We cannot do this for someone else but as we change ourselves, as we unfold those higher qualities that will not allow us to hurt another, we are helping the collective to change too because instead of negative vibes going from us the positivity will flow and this will affect others to perhaps change themselves. The process almost reverberates.

Our indoctrination may mean that we have a bias against a particular race or religion, but we can only change ourselves. When we come to that understanding we can see in our reaction to that scenario that we didn't realize we were so prejudiced or biased. We may ask 'Where is this coming from? Is it indoctrination or is it something that I've just carried with me?' That's when we can work on ourselves.

## **By recognizing and accepting the journey of the soul through the Cycles, Rounds and Ages.**

We are coming to the end of the Piscean Age which has lasted 2,400 or so years. We're now on the threshold of the Aquarian Age. At the end of every great Age more souls incarnate in order to transmute the karma of that Age. Therefore, it is not surprising that there are so many Souls struggling with health, conflict, chaos. They are working out the karma of the lives experienced during the Piscean Age.

If we study Metaphysics, Theosophy and Cosmogenesis we know that we are in the 4$^{th}$ Round of Earth. There's the Cosmos, the Solar Systems and the Planetary Systems. We're in the 2$^{nd}$ Solar System and in each Solar System there are Cycles, Rounds of Earth and Ages. The journey of the soul goes through all these and we accumulate karma and soul lessons throughout. Therefore, it is by recognizing that we are more than just the body that you see here and now, that we are all old souls. We've come through many different Ages and Cycles and Rounds. This is the Experiment of Creation and we just keep on going from one Cycle to another. The acceptance that we are more than what we see here today is what is important. There is a greater Self that we probably know very little about, but we are part of all that.

How do we deal with the consequences of recognizing and transmuting karma? We can just sit back and do nothing but accept this. Indeed, nothing's going to happen to us if we make this decision; just let life happen. But if we like studying and we want to understand more there's books and teachers out there to help us do that.

## **By working with the Elements within ourselves**

What are the elements within us? We know the natural elements are Earth, Air, Fire and Water. We recognize and work with the Elements within ourselves. What is Water? These are our emotions. When we are working with our emotions, we are working with the water element. All the Elements within us need to be balanced. What is Fire? - Love and Aspiration. Where do we have that? In our hearts. What is the Earth? - The physical body. Earth is our body, we stand rooted to the Earth. What's the Air? – It is the mind and our thoughts.

It's understanding ourselves and how each element within us needs to be balanced. This can be done by understanding ourselves, what we're made of. Outside the ancient temples there used to be a winged disc, saying, 'Man know thyself and thou shall know the Universe.' Everything in the Universe is here, the Elements are within us. Our work is to balance them. The fire of love is also a force and that's why the heart is the balancing point within us. The lower chakras are wonderful because they're helping us to transmute and evolve from the past. We are helped in this by the higher mind and the chakras within the head. This is the higher consciousness, so all the chakras are working together, there's no separation from them. We are not only working on one chakra because everything is blended, and everything has to work together. That's when those beautiful discs spin brighter and faster.

## **By remembering that the very essence that moves the Universe is also within us.**

Forget all about karma, forget about everything else. If we were to remember this jewel of truth we would be liberated from all that holds us back. If only we could touch on that one essential Truth that the very essence that moves the Universe is also within us then all our problems would be over and we wouldn't need to be here. It is the Law of Connectedness. It all comes back to the 12 Laws. Our actions are visible, but we keep our thoughts and feelings to ourselves. What we don't realize is that our thoughts affect other people and what is around us. If we remember and live by the Laws we can change things, we can make life so much better. Just think that instead of feeling depressed or fearful about what's happening in the world we just send out thoughts of love and light. If each one of us sends out thoughts of love and light to the world, just letting the Higher Beings take those thoughts of goodness out into the world, think how much we can change.

The Laws of Creation are wonderful. Everything has a fundamental meaning. We are not yet one with nature. Butterflies will fly because they are at one with nature. It's not a matter of choice it's about oneness. We have yet to reach that oneness with the laws of nature. We are responsible for all that happens in the world; the natural disasters happen because of our actions and thoughts. The best we can do to address that is to send thoughts of healing, love and compassion to those affected areas to hold nature in balance. We cannot neglect that by thinking that it's nothing to do with us because it's on the other side of the world; that might be the cause and effect for that particular region but also it is sending us the message of 'You have an opportunity now to do something about this, so what are you going to do?'

We can't get away from the fact that we're all connected. It gives us the opportunity to do something even if it's just sending out the Light. With something like Facebook for example, people very often don't stop and think, they just react and on Facebook it's so much easier to do that because you're not looking at someone, it's just a machine and what you say and how you say it is less controlled and people can go to town in expressing their anger or whatever. Everything comes back to how well do we know ourselves.

Do not confuse the Law of Karma with the Law of Retribution. The Law of Karma is just and fair. The Law of Karma offers you the opportunity to transmute it by understanding, by an act of love, by an act of compassion so the Law of Karma can be transmuted. What about the Law of Retribution? What does retribution really mean? Retribution says, 'You will pay'. Perhaps we have had a number of lifetimes when our personality has refused to acknowledge our Soul and has preferred doing evil acts to others and does not wish to learn to move on. Some souls can stay in the darkness for several lifetimes and if we continue to do evil, it is then that the Law of Retribution acts as part of balancing karma. We have got to reach a point where we understand that what we have done is against the Law of Love.

When the soul gets to the stage where finally they get it, 'I've done some awful things in the past' and if the soul is then humbled and has the humility to say 'I'm really sorry, I understand now the evil or wrong that I have caused' and we follow this with acts of goodness, so contrition is expressed in action, that's when we can transmute that karma. But until it learns that it continues adding possibly more and more difficult karma to its debits. It is about all of us recognizing the connectedness of all life within us. It's not one law for the rich and another for the poor, the laws are for everyone and rich and poor are only for one lifetime. It's what we create in our being and living that matters, not what is in the bank account. Humanity is truly evolving through the chakras and receiving amazing opportunities to learn.

The karmic process is transformative, constantly alchemizing evil into good, pain and suffering into joy and happiness. Spiritual Laws are just and fair!

We need to go back to heal the original wound. We all have a life way back somewhere which started the drum roll of karma and that's where the original wound comes from. If we could go back to that lifetime and heal it then everything else would follow like a domino effect. Where did it all start, where did it all come from? Our soul will know this.

It always comes down to the absence of love, self-love because if we reject our own love we wound ourselves. The answer is that we need to remember who we are. It also links to connectedness. We have to remember the very essence of who we are, and that very essence is the light and love that we are. Fear is not knowing ourselves and thinking someone else is better than we are. It also all comes back to the chakras as well and not really understanding our chakras. Fear is at the root of everything and is humanity's greatest enemy.

## CHAPTER 9

# Healing with the Ancestors – Our Spiritual Dna

When we speak of our spiritual DNA, we are not just speaking of our earthly ancestors, of our current family history. We are speaking of our Ancestral Group Soul. So how do we define the Ancestral Group Soul? This is about the history of our Soul. Being part of an ancestral group soul takes us beyond the immediate family history. Indeed, some people feel very little connection with their earthly family whilst other know that there is a deep affinity between them. On both counts we may have taken on continued group karma. We are all aspects of a greater group Soul. It is the group Soul that knows the plan and purpose for our unfoldment.

The Ancestral Group Soul is made up of facets or aspects and develops along the planetary life, the ray on which it was created, the life-stream, the root-race, the initiation it is experiencing, the soul lessons and the spiritual qualities it is unfolding. As each aspect or facet develops the understanding, purpose and quality of the whole group is building and unfolding the knowledge of the ancestral group soul. By embracing this knowledge, it could lead us to the conclusion that our ancestors live through us as it is a natural progression of evolution. As aspects of something greater than ourselves, as we evolve, as we learn and unfold our own spiritual qualities, so are the ancestral group soul unfolding and learning too. This means that through us our ancestral group soul continues its journey through one lifetime after another. So perhaps the next question is 'Are we our

Ancestors, and will our descendants be us? Is this then the eternal life? That we continue, albeit in different bodies, but the soul memory the consciousness continues to evolve and grow until we reach that point of the Crown Chakra - I KNOW THAT I AM.

With the realisation of there being something greater than ourselves, we could also realise that perhaps a condition or health problem has manifested because of a soul dis-harmony, lessons unlearned, in previous lives. If we accept that we are all part of an ancestral group soul, could our problem, our condition be taken back to our group? What understanding can we get from all this? Wise teachers tell us that all diseases are a manifestation of soul dis-ease, a soul dis-harmony. Therefore, we need to go back to our ancestral group soul to try to figure it out.

Our spiritual DNA is not about producing exacting results at a molecular and cellular level. It is about understanding our ancestry at soul and spiritual level. It is about the understanding of who we are and what part we play in the unfolding purpose of humanity. Our lives are not just about 'plain little me', our lives are integrated with something far greater than ourselves. If this is so, how come we are not aware of this? Very simply, it is the experience of our lives and conditions that is enabling that group soul to evolve. There are other aspects too developing and unfolding through their own experience, enriching the whole group. If we knew or were aware of others, then our reaction to our experiences would be influenced by this knowledge and our soul can only progress by our own reaction and how we deal with that experience.

So our contact with the ancestors and our quest for our spiritual DNA lies in the acceptance and acknowledgment that there is something far greater than 'little me'. Once we realise and understand the depth of our very being, acknowledging the presence of the ancestors is not so difficult. The difficulty lies with the 'outer mind' letting go.

To honour our ancestors, we must first honour ourselves. Not just as the individual we see in the mirror each day, but as the soul that is behind the Light shining from our eyes. It is this acceptance of the soul that will eventually help us to recognise our true being. It is this understanding that will eventually give credence to the essence of our being. This understanding, this knowledge comes with self-realisation. We may read many books, go to many lectures and workshops and listen to many teachers and we may acquire knowledge of the mind, but until we have realised TRUTH in our hearts, we will never really 'know' – this is our inner knowledge, this is gnosis.

It is through the soul memory that we are able to contact the ancestral group soul. The ancestors are there to help us. Through their own experiences, they have given us many gifts, many qualities. We live with these gifts and these qualities in our everyday lives, but yet we may not be aware of this. These are our spiritual genes. What we do with them is up to us. It is our own experiences that enhance these genes. As we develop and unfold our spiritual qualities through the lessons we learn from everyday life, so are we enriching the very essence of our ancestral group soul. When we begin to realise that the soul is who we truly are, we also realise that the personality is not an enemy to our growth. The personality is the servant of the soul; it is the vehicle through which the soul can express itself. The more we allow this to happen, the more that we are expressing our divinity into the world.

We are not separate from God; we are rather integral parts of God – we are co-creators with the Divine Will. Our enlightenment does not come by a gift from God; it comes from our well-earned lessons throughout our soul's journey and history. Enlightenment means becoming the radiant divine self that we are, once we have shed the cloak of the personality.

Our motivation comes with the knowledge that we are Eternal; that there never has been a time when we have not been spirit. In this realisation we can take comfort that whatever life may throw at us, we have that inner depth, that inner strength to cope and overcome.

This is a time when humanity is awakening. It is awakening to its true potential, to a spiritual dimension deep within. It may not always understand or know what that potential is, but it senses that there is so much more than one life. We are part of something greater. The Soul of Humanity is awakening to its real 'I AM', to its real consciousness. We are awakening to our collective soul – a group soul. It has learned through its history of collective experiences; it has expressed itself through different races, religions, cultures and it is now awaiting its moment to sense, through the miasma of human diversity, that inner unity. It is through the richness of our differences, our diversity that we will recognise who we are and unite in true brotherhood.

The soul of humanity is seeking to inculcate a higher set of values into us. Whilst this is a period of real painful adjustments for so many, it is also a time when humanity is entering a more enlightened period. This is a time when we can measure ourselves by how we deal with crisis and conflict. For it is by going through those moments of crisis and conflict that we really find out who we are.

So how can we support the Soul of Humanity? How can we live up to that higher potential, those higher values? We can support humanity's Oneness by honouring diversity. We can understand that there is always a dual purpose behind all that is happening to us and around us, and globally. The duality is our material and spiritual life – our Soul and our personality. We therefore need to look beyond the outer form, the personality, so that we can discern the Truth that the Soul is trying to teach us. It's not about black and white, or good and evil, with deeper knowledge we see that life is a mixture of both.

It's also important to remember that not one individual, not one nation, not one religion has found the only Truth. But each may have found an aspect of the Truth.

Humanity has entered a great period of crisis on the road to enlightenment. We are facing enormous challenges and yet this is not a time to either show fear or despair about our future. It is merely a period of more testing and lessons to be learned.

The Soul of Humanity – our great group soul is moving forward and seeking greater expression in the material world.

This is truly a time of transformation, a great happening in the history of Souls. We all have the responsibility to play our part.

Let us do so with courage, with understanding and above all with unconditional love.

Individually, as our chakras or centres develop, this is also unfolding the understanding, purpose and quality of our individual soul antahkarana. This is the Bridge that connects the lower to the higher (the personality to the soul, and the soul to the spirit). The antahkarana gives us deeper insight, something that the outer mind, the personality may not always be able to fathom. We need to realise that there is a soul purpose behind each ailment. So what is that purpose and how can we find this out?

To try to discover that purpose we need to be very clear and honest with ourselves. We all have deep connections with the Ancestral Group Soul. The connection goes back aeons; therefore, the current problem or condition may also go back some time, through successive lifetimes. Our Ancestors are willing to help us to understand so that we may, in our own time, learn how to deal with and heal the condition or problem that we may be facing. With knowledge also comes deep responsibility. Whilst healing ourselves is of course beneficial to us personally, we need to be aware that we are also dealing with group karma and we need to be responsible and, in some ways, sacrificial in how we deal with the problem. There needs to be a very specific purpose and intention in our meditative process. Remember too that all conditions have a deeper soul meaning. We can try to link and work with the ancestors and ask for their help.

**So, commence by asking these questions:**

- Why do you want to do this?
- Have you ever felt a connection to an ancestral group?
- What is the current problem?
- Is it physical, mental, emotional, spiritual?
- Have you ever been conscious that you belong to something far greater than yourself?
- Have you ever been conscious of helpers, guides, angels?

- Have you ever been aware of a presence – a gentle guidance around you?
- Is it a genetic disease?
- Is it a family repetitive pattern?
- Is it affecting other family members?
- Go beyond the medical/scientific reasoning
- Can the current problem be related to a particular Chakra?

**We need to remember:**

- That there may be deeper soul responsibilities.
- Be respectful and aware of sacred space and contracts at soul level
- Honour the Ancestors
- Accept your place in that Group Soul
- Give thanks to them
- Be open to receive
- Be willing to co-operate
- Be willing to change
- Be understanding, our family ancestors were also doing their best
- Our ancestors do not want us to stay stuck/trapped in the past
- No guilt, no blame, just the need to acknowledge, to accept, to heal and move on
- Give ourselves permission to be free and release ourselves

**A simple meditative process to follow:**
**Preparation time:**

- Start by writing down what your purpose is by wishing to call upon the ancestors
- Prepare yourself physically
- Prepare yourself emotionally and mentally
- Prepare your space
- Switch off phones, make sure you will not be disturbed
- Be very clear as to your intention
- Don't ask for too many things at once

- Start breathing exercises – the in and out breath going deeper with each breath
- Slowly and gently attune yourself to the Light
- Raise your awareness to that centre of peace and stillness within you
- Then, when you are feeling at peace and still within
- Ask for your guide or guardian angel to be present to help you
- Feel their strong support around you, then
- Ask and invite the ancestors to join you
- Allow this to happen naturally
- When you feel or see a presence ask for help and understanding about your problem
- Wait – let go of all pre-thoughts and requests
- Accept – whatever comes
- When you feel that enough has been done for one day, then
- Give thanks to the 'ancestor', 'helper' and start closing down
- Give thanks overall for the guidance and protection received
- Seal yourself

Be very firm and start using the breath to connect again with your physical body.

It's important to be aware that our ancestors may only be able to show us symbolically what they are trying to share. Please do not get upset if nothing appears to be clear or indeed if nothing is happening. There are always reasons for this. Perhaps we are too anxious and thereby putting up blocks (*even if we may not be aware of this*). We need also to be aware that our interpretation of what we have been given may be clouded by our own sub-conscious or perception.

***The essential thing is that we have asked – perhaps in their own time, when we least expect it, the answer will come.***

**When you have finished - SEAL YOUR CENTRES** (*extremely important*)

It is vitally important that you always seal your centres after you have done a process on yourself. A very simple sealing to do is thus:

Imagine a cross of light encircled by light (+) and place this on your Chakras: Crown, Brow, Throat, Heart, Solar Plexus, Sacral, Root.

Then imagine a Circle of Light all round your body (*as if you were enclosed in a bubble of light*).

Finally, see a straight a shaft of Light coming from the Crown of your head, down through your body and down to your feet, earthing you, grounding you.

If you feel the need for extra grounding, please put your hands in cold water and sprinkle some water around your head area. If, after the above, you still feel a little light headed and not quite yourself – have a shower.

**Enjoy your time with the Ancestors**

## CHAPTER 10

# The Spirit

Spirit is pure essence. It is our very breath, the energy that sustains us. This essence was breathed out from the Absolute Being and sustains all Creation. The Absolute Being breathed out an energy, a fire and life eventually (after aeons and aeons of time) became form. These forms were the initial constellations, planets, cosmic life, solar life and planetary life that we know about. We are all Spirit. There never has been a time when we were not spirit as this is the very essence of our Being. It is our prime motivator. It is the I AM. From the moment that we were breathed forth from the Creator, the Absolute Being, we were pure Spirit. The Universe is motivated by this pure essence, this energy.

We need to understand that this initial impulse, this breathing forth was the very beginning of our existence. Spirit has no form – it is pure energy. Think of those three words

EXPERIMENT    EXPERIENCE    EXPRESSION

Life itself was the initial experiment. But in order to experience itself, it breathed forth impulses into myriads of forms. Initially we are talking about constellations, stars and planets. It is said there were also seven breaths, thus the seven Major Rays. There have been different Solar and Planetary systems. From these have existed Chains, Globes, Rounds and Root-races.

However, spirit has no form so it needed a vehicle to experience itself. That is what is known as the Soul consciousness. It is the Soul consciousness, through the experiences of the personality over many, many lifetimes, that is able to express the very essence of Spirit. The very purpose of our lives is to unfold those inherent spiritual qualities to their highest degree.

The whole of Creation is an experiment – an experience that can only be measured by the myriad of forms' expressions,

# CHAPTER 11

# ....and so the journey continues...

The beauty of life is that there is no ending. The Soul will know when it is the right time to leave its physical body. Maybe we have learned our life's lessons, maybe not. However, the beauty of life is that we get more opportunities to learn whatever we have left unfinished in any one lifetime.

This is the journey of the Soul. It is created, it lives, it gathers the harvest and then plants the seed for the next lifetime. Thus, ever growing, ever unfolding. The going is often tough, it is unyielding because Saturn will ensure that we learn those lessons really, really well. It will not allow us to skip over any lessons. If we don't get it right the first time then we keep coming back until we do.

The Planets, the Rays are there to influence us and assist us in unfolding our true self. Every soul has to incarnate in all the signs of the zodiac in order to learn the soul lessons of each sign. This does not mean that we only have twelve lives. We may have hundreds of lives. We continue to incarnate in any particular sign until we have fully learned the soul lesson.

But why worry? Life is eternal and there is no hurry. The journey of the Soul can be an adventure, the greatest we can ever undertake.

The Soul continues its path through the different Ages, Cycles and Root-races. We are all part of this Cosmic dance through many different expressions.

CPSIA information can be obtained
at www.ICGtesting.com
Printed in the USA
BVHW030848120919
558266BV00001B/122/P

9 781982 228576